Letters to the Future
A Simple Guide for Writing Your Memoir

P.M. Martin

Letters to the Future

A Simple Guide for Writing Your Memoir

ISBN: 9780997842753

Letters to the Future: The Simple Guide for Writing Your Memoir

DEDICATION

IN LOVING MEMORY OF PATRICK

I WISH I HAD COLLECTED HIS STORIES BEFORE HE PASSED

Why Write a Memoir?

What were your ancestors' lives like? When did your grandparents fall in love? Did your father ask permission to propose to your mother? Did your great aunt keep a victory garden during the war? Does your family have a history of collecting rare books, hiking through the woods, or keeping bees? Did you get your love of needlework from your mother who got it from her grandmother?

Imagine knowing the personal details about your friends and family, especially narratives from the past. Collecting and sharing your personal stories gives a sense of connection, affinity, and belonging to young people. When you take the time to preserve the stories from your life, you not only save your stories for the future but help your friends and family to better connect to you.

I wrote this book because:

My student Emily struggles to capture on paper the incredible events of her life.

My sister Mary wants to share the tales of her children's days of growing up.

My Aunt Michal is the keeper of Patrick's stories and of their colorful childhood in Northern Indiana.

My Aunt Mary Jane and Uncle Jim hold the recollections of generations in their memories, which I want to pass on to my kids.

My father-in-law is one of the last of the great men of the Baby Boomers; his stories are valuable.

And because I want to read the memories, the tales, the dreams, and the aspirations of the people most important to me. I want to coax those stories from them so I can appreciate them.

I hope this guide can support you on your journey to collect and preserve your personal stories to pass onto loved ones who will cherish them.

Your Unique Story is Your Most Valuable Treasure

Have you considered writing a memoir or passing the chronicles of your life on to your children, grandchildren, or extended family and friends? Is there someone in your life whose history you would like to record? Have you attempted to write down your stories, only to find the process too challenging? Sometimes, we can become distracted or overwhelmed by life and find it difficult to write down the words we want to pass on to our loved ones.

The task of collecting personal stories into a memoir can be daunting for anyone. Many people are not sure where to start. Some get distracted by busy lives or become worried that others will judge their writing, and many give up after a short time, leaving the project unfinished.

Our stories are our greatest treasures and the most valuable legacies we can leave our loved ones. When we pass on our stories, we pass on a sense of heritage, belonging, and an understanding of the past. People are naturally curious about their ancestors, family, and friends. They want to know about childhood nicknames, personal hobbies, and impactful experiences.

After my dad passed, I visited with my Aunt Michal for a weekend. I learned more about him by listening to her stories than I had in the years he and I lived together. It was during that visit that I realized the importance of collecting personal narratives from our loved ones.

Our stories outlive us.

Although the thought of writing your memoir may feel intimidating, this guide will help you document some of your most valuable experiences to share with your loved ones.

How to Use this Book

This book is to be used as a guide to help you in writing down your meaningful experiences. In this book, you simply answer the prompts to construct your memoir. You are welcome to skip around, change the prompts, expand as much as you would like, and add details where it suits you. You can use this guide to tell your personal story that can be passed on to friends and family. Once finished, give the completed book to your children, grandchildren, or friends, knowing they will care for your stories and safeguard them for future generations.

This book also can be used as a discussion guide. Use it to interview those whose stories you want to collect. Record the details of their lives onto the pages of this book by using the prompts as conversation starters. Many of us do not know how to start the conversation to collect stories from our family members, but this guide offers direction by providing the questions to ask.

For each of the writing prompts, elaborate with as much depth and detail as you can. Keep in mind that your friends and family reading your stories will understand the stories better if you describe all of the little details, so try to be thorough. Use sensory details (sight, sound, texture, taste, and smell) to create a clear memory. The more depth and detail, the better.

The prompts in the first section of the book are more specific and ask for particular details, but the later prompts are open-ended to encourage more freedom in writing. Feel free to answer each question in the direction that best suits you.

Take your time as you collect your stories in one place—this book. Your loved ones will appreciate that you saved your most valuable treasures for them to cherish.

What is in a Name?

What was your full name at birth and what is your name now? What does your name mean? Do you like it? Why did your parents name you that? What did people call you when you were a child? When you were a teenager? Did you ever have a nickname? What was it, and how did you get it?

_____

_____

_____

_____

_____

_____

_____

_____

_____

_____

_____

_____

_____

_____

_____

_____

_____

_____

_____

_____

_____

_____

_____

_____

_____

_____

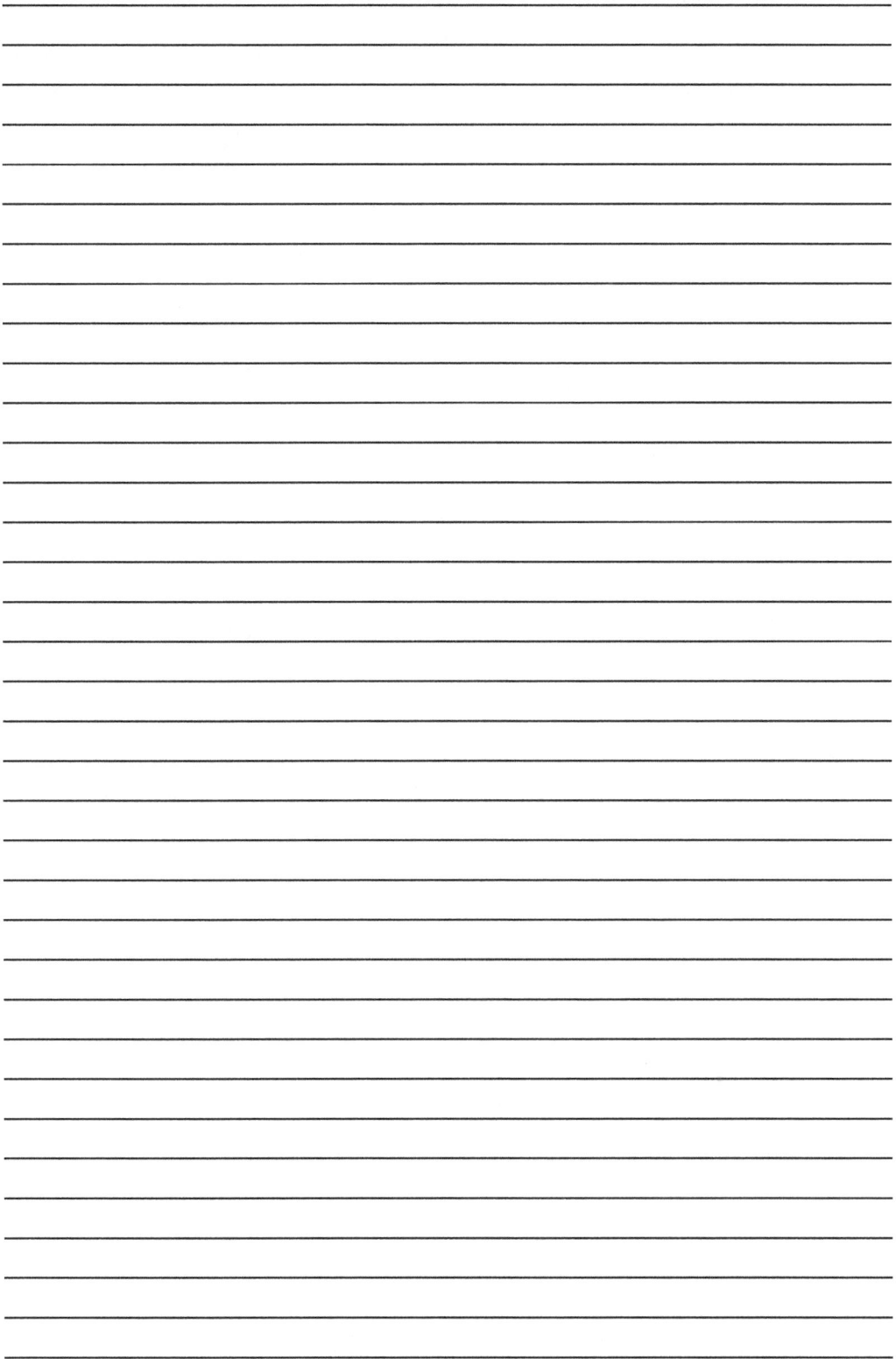

Family and First Friends

What are the names and birthdays of your parents? What are your favorite memories with your parents? What three words would you use to describe them and why? Did you look up to your parents when you were a kid? What did you admire about them? What about them irritated you?

Who are your siblings? What were they like as kids? How did you get along as kids? What is your favorite memory with your siblings (or cousins or friends) when you were young? Which kid were you--the smart one, the attractive one, the athletic one, etc.? Why did you get that label?

_____

_____

_____

_____

_____

_____

_____

_____

_____

_____

_____

_____

_____

_____

_____

_____

_____

_____

_____

_____

_____

_____

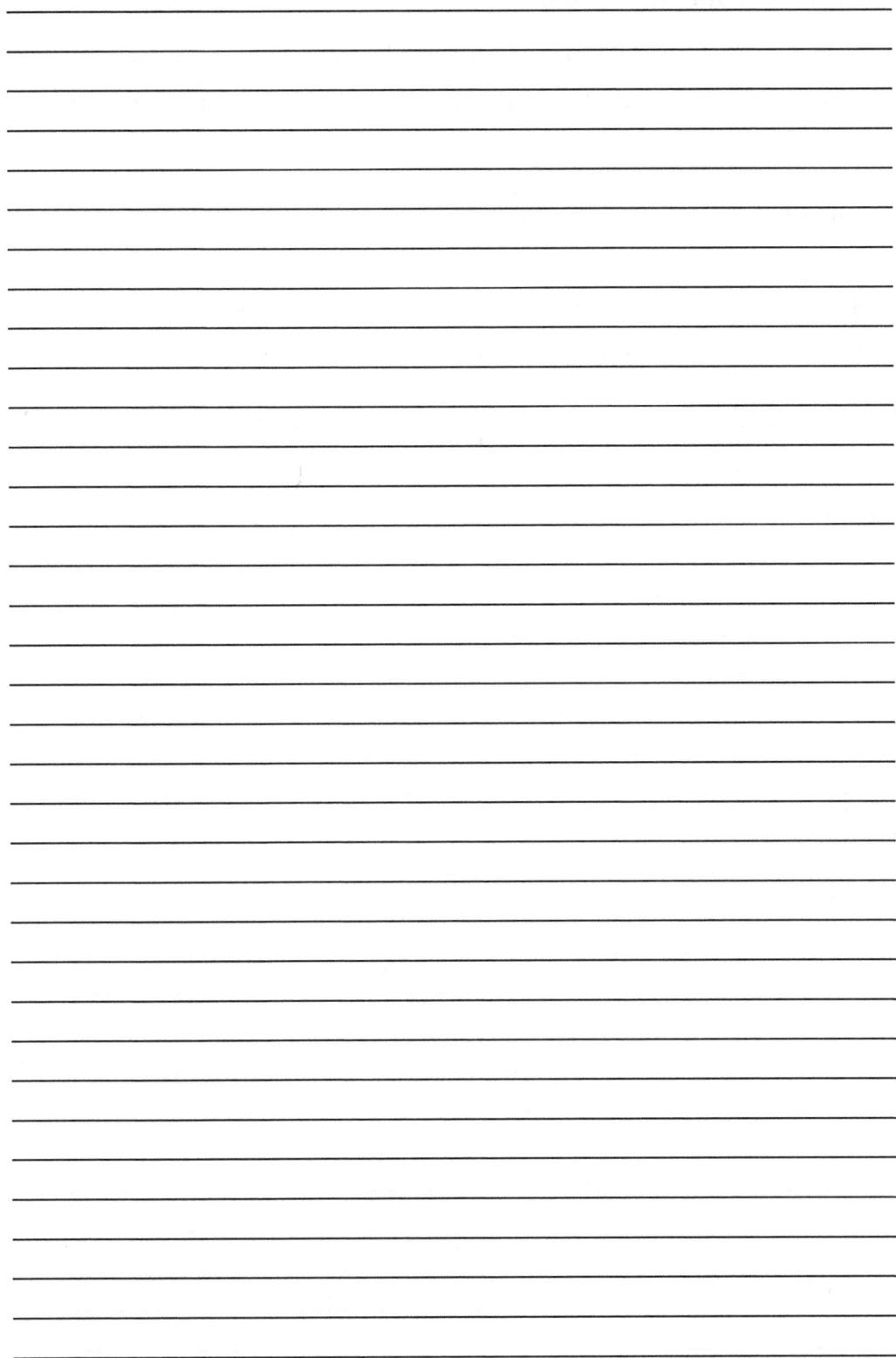

Who Were Your Ancestors?

What are the names and birthdates of your grandparents? What are some interesting things you remember about them? What were their personalities, favorite activities, and memories you shared?

How about your great-grandparents, aunts, uncles, cousins, or other relatives? Do you know their names and birthplaces? What were their occupations? Did you ever meet them? What did you hear about them from others? What about them did you like? What stories did they tell you about their past and where they came from?

Do you know any ancestors' names, birthdays, or places of birth prior to your great-grandparents? What countries and cultures did your ancestors come from? Is that important to you? If so, why?

_____

_____

_____

_____

_____

_____

_____

_____

_____

_____

_____

_____

_____

_____

_____

_____

_____

_____

_____

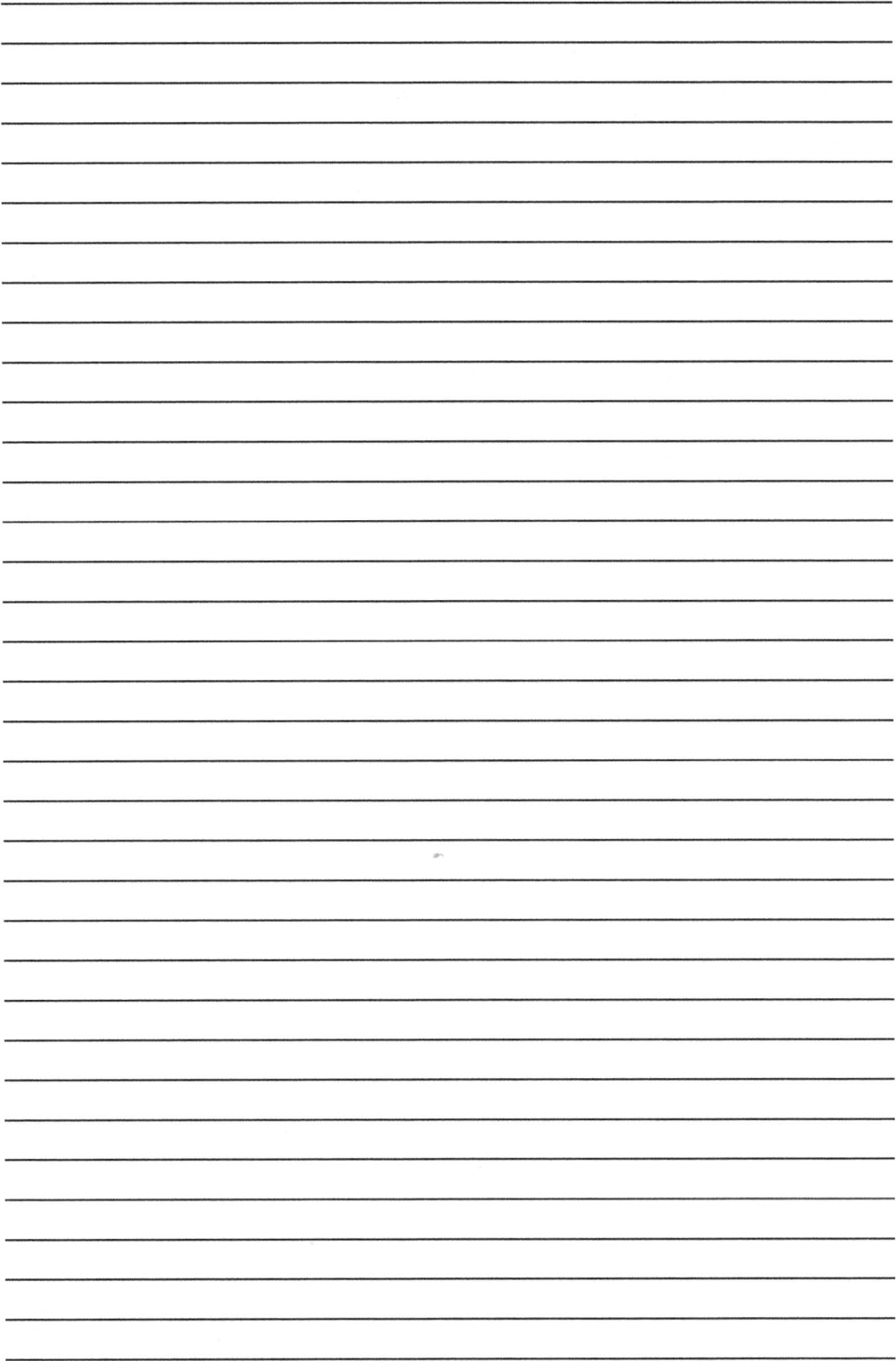

A Snapshot of Childhood

Attach a photograph of yourself when you were young and explain it below. This could be a school picture, a holiday family photo, or a snapshot of a family vacation. Explain what it is, where you got it, what event it is connected to, and its importance.

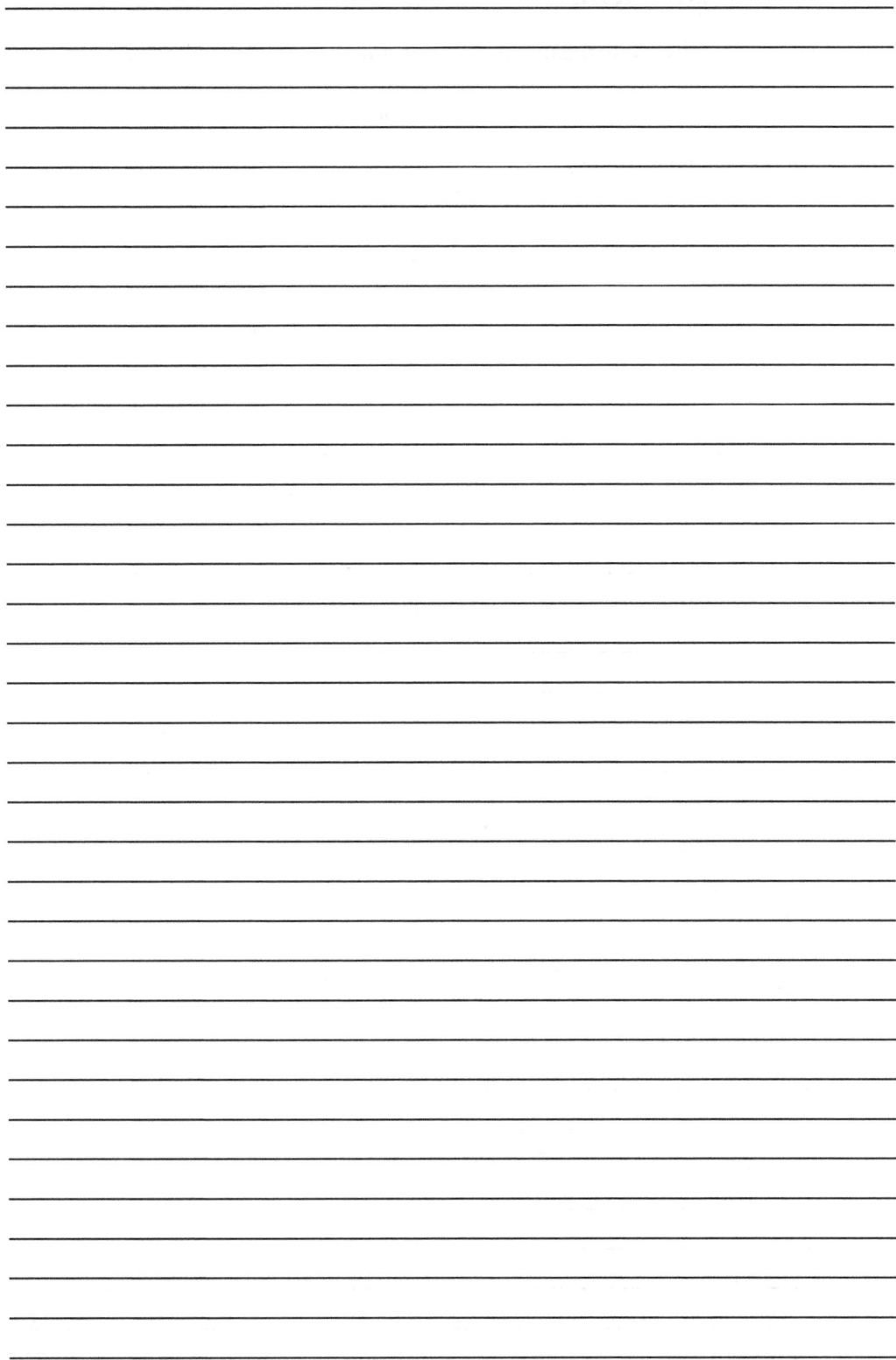

Family Name and Heritage

What does your family name mean? Is it important to you? Are you proud of it?

From what country or culture does your name originate? Is that significant to you? Why or why not? Have you traced the genealogy of your family's history? What did you learn? Do you have any stories about your family's culture of origin? Which of your ancestors immigrated? Why did they immigrate?

Share your thoughts, opinions, or a story about your family's background, name, or ancestors.

_____

_____

_____

_____

_____

_____

_____

_____

_____

_____

_____

_____

_____

_____

_____

_____

_____

_____

_____

_____

_____

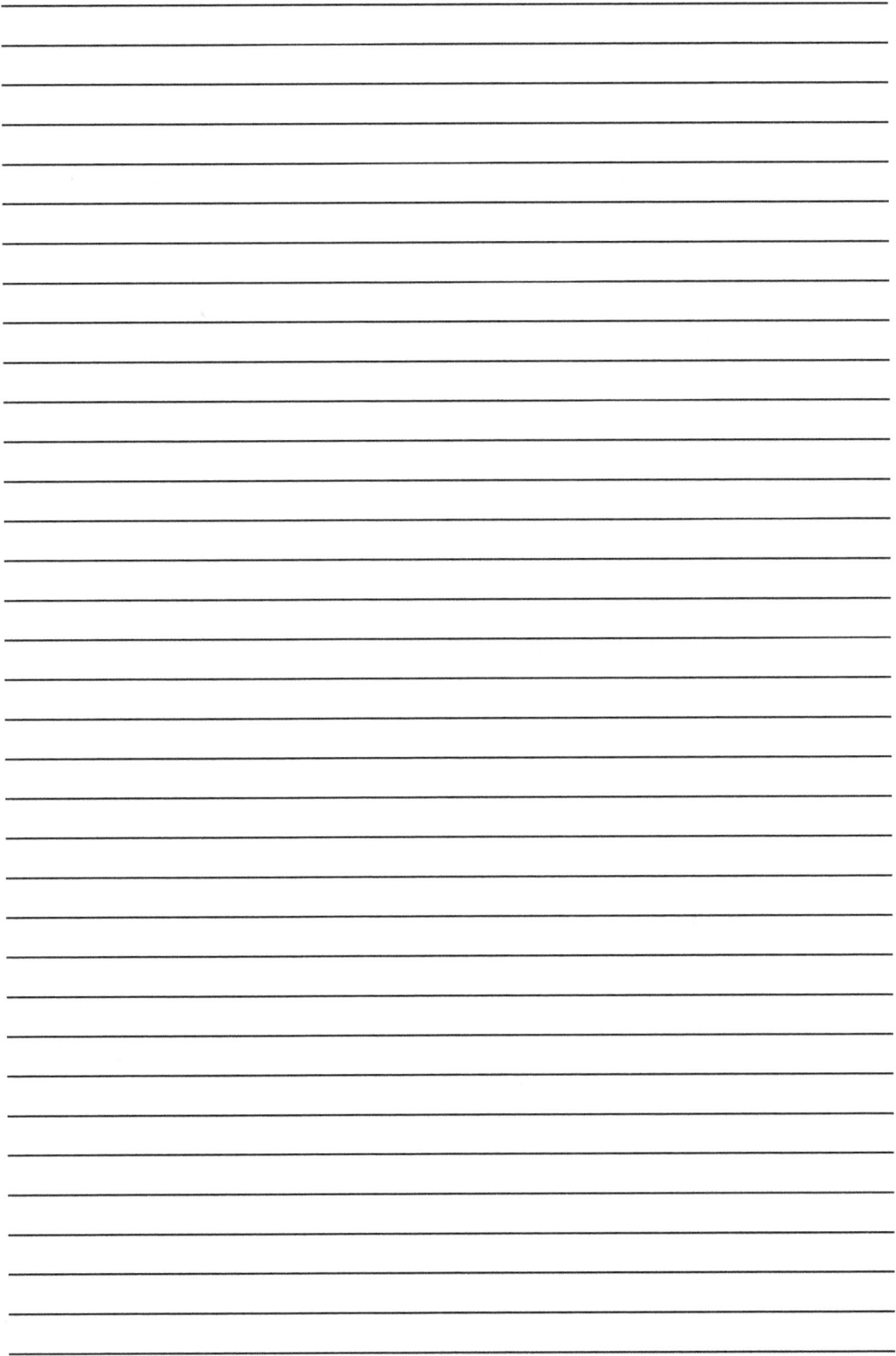

Childhood Hometown

Where did you grow up? Describe what it was like there—the weather, the people, and the culture. What events did you look forward to each year? What did you like about it? What elements made it special? What house from your early childhood stands out to you? Describe how it looked, felt, smelled, and even sounded. Who visited or what happened there to make it important? What is the best memory of being in the place where you grew up?

_____
_____
_____
_____
_____
_____
_____
_____
_____
_____
_____
_____
_____
_____
_____
_____
_____
_____
_____
_____
_____
_____
_____
_____
_____

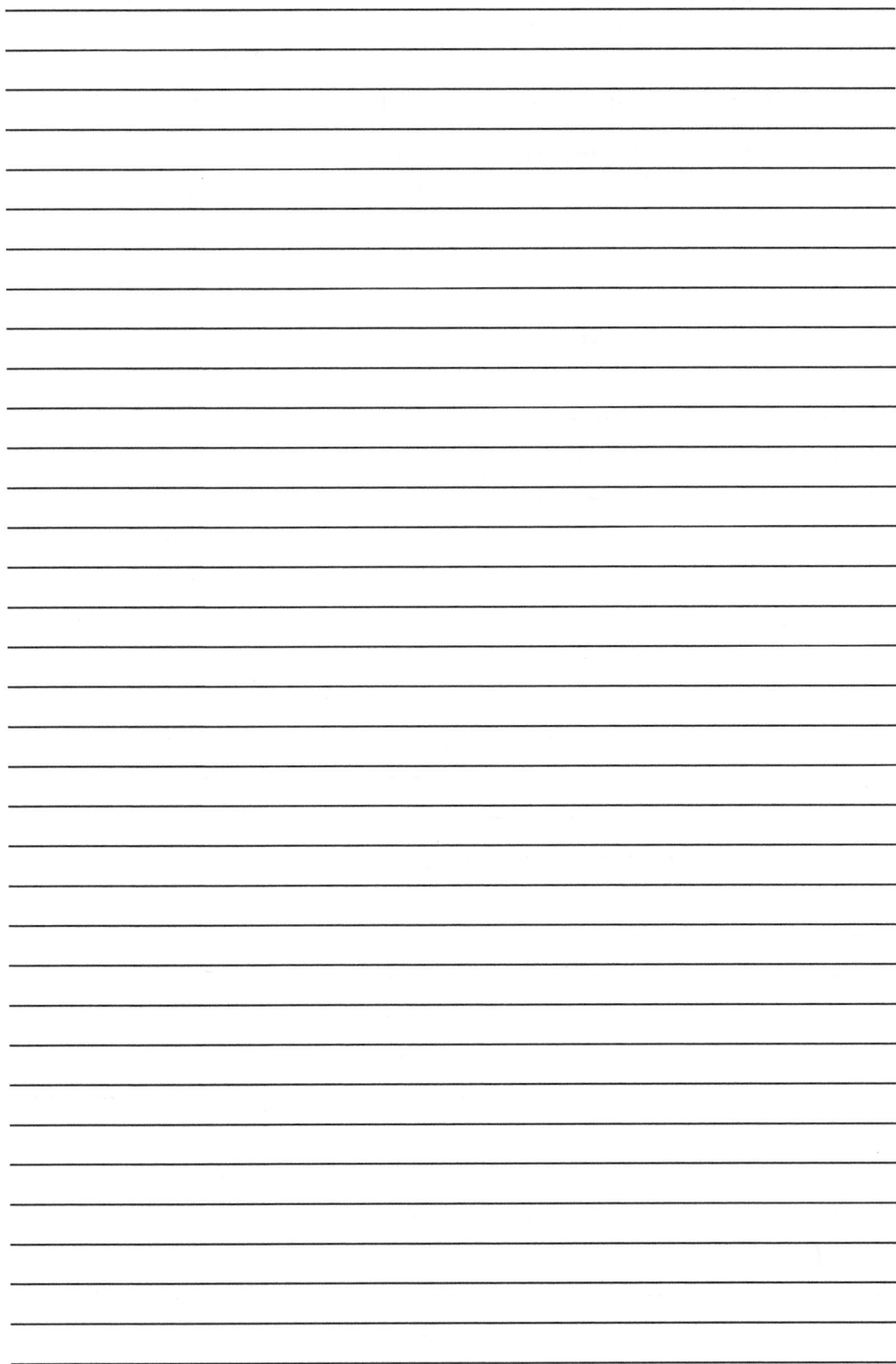

A Child's Favorite Things

When you were a little kid, what were your favorite belongings (toys, clothes, blankets, stuffed animals, or photographs)? What were your favorite books or stories growing up? Who were your closest friends? What were your favorite activities? When you were birth to 5 years old, what did you most like to do? Who was your favorite teacher? What memory stands out the most during your elementary years? Do you recall elementary school being a magical time of exploration or a time of drudgery and boredom?

_____
_____
_____
_____
_____
_____
_____
_____
_____
_____
_____
_____
_____
_____
_____
_____
_____
_____
_____
_____
_____
_____
_____
_____

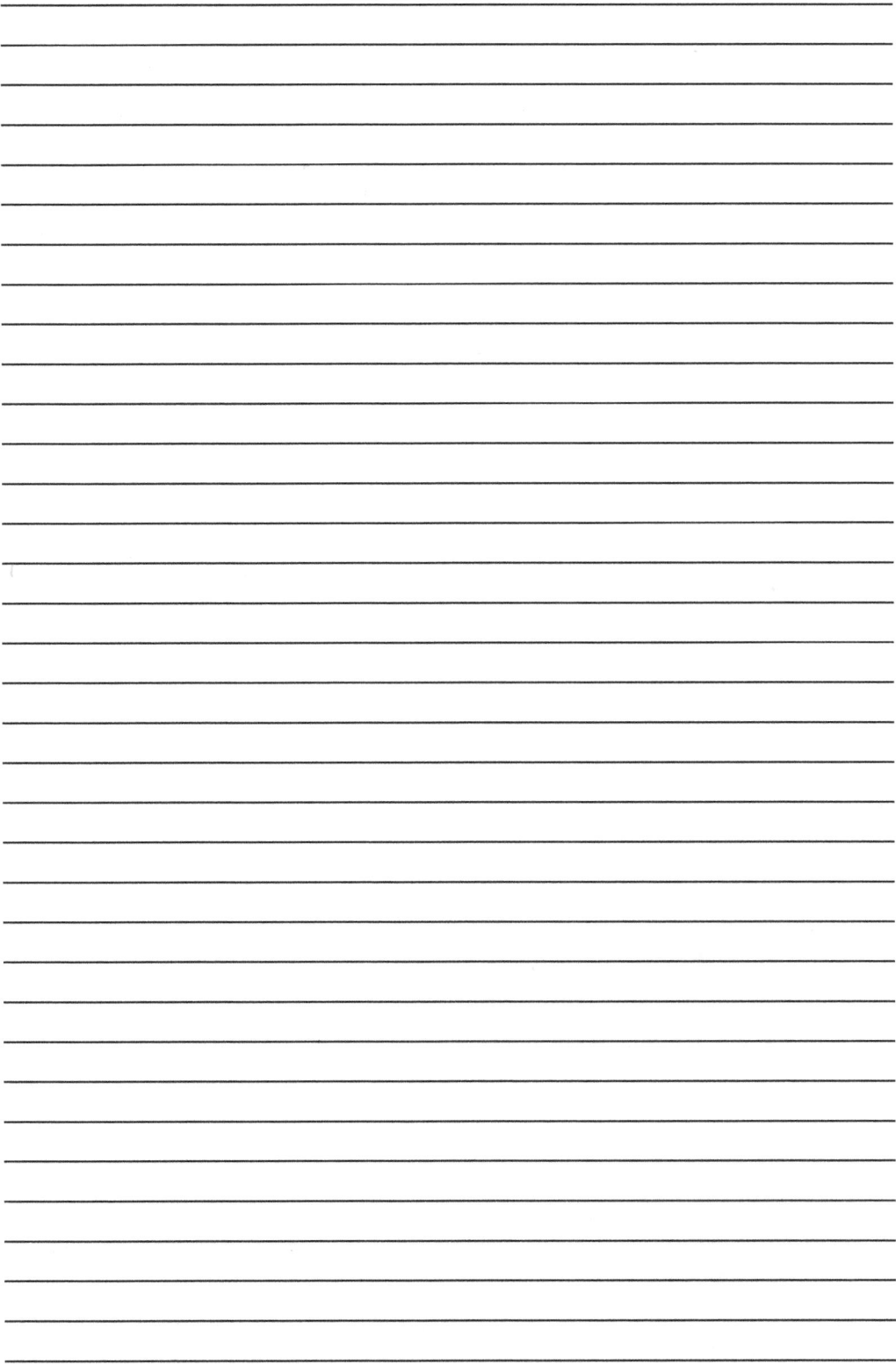

What Did You Want to Be?

Describe your favorite characters from books, TV, or movies when you were a kid.
As a child, what did you want to be when you grew up? When you were a little kid,
what was your outlook on life? Did you tend to think of the world as a place of
limitless possibility or a bureaucracy of annoying rules? Who was the rule keeper in
your house? Who was the parent who always said "yes"? How did your parents (or
other people) support your dreams?

_____

_____

_____

_____

_____

_____

_____

_____

_____

_____

_____

_____

_____

_____

_____

_____

_____

_____

_____

_____

_____

_____

_____

_____

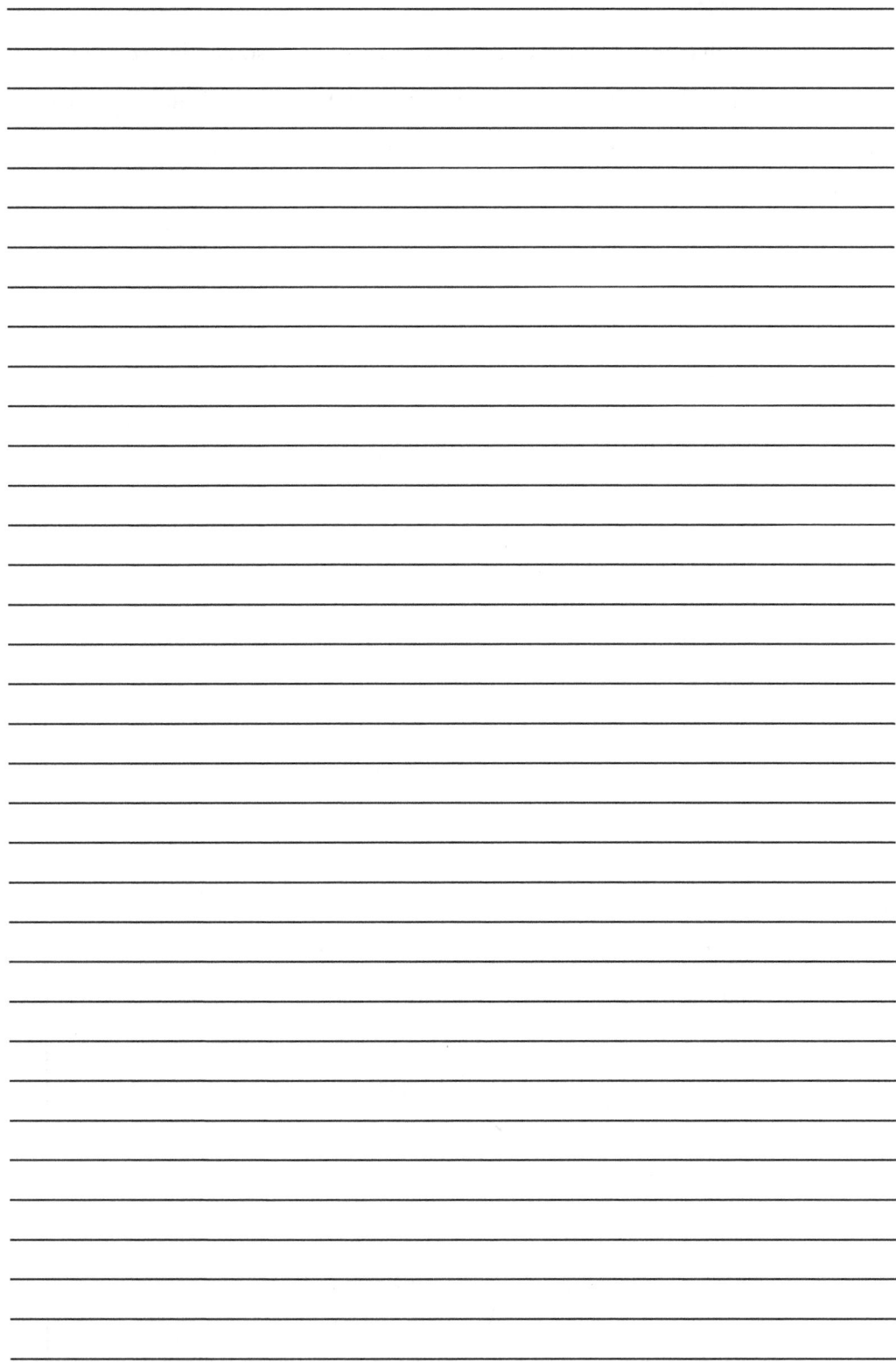

An Image of Days Gone By

Attach a picture, drawing, or piece of artwork of yourself or something you did when you were a young person. This might be a piece of art you created, an image that was special to you, or a class picture of you in school. Explain the image, when it was taken, and why it is important.

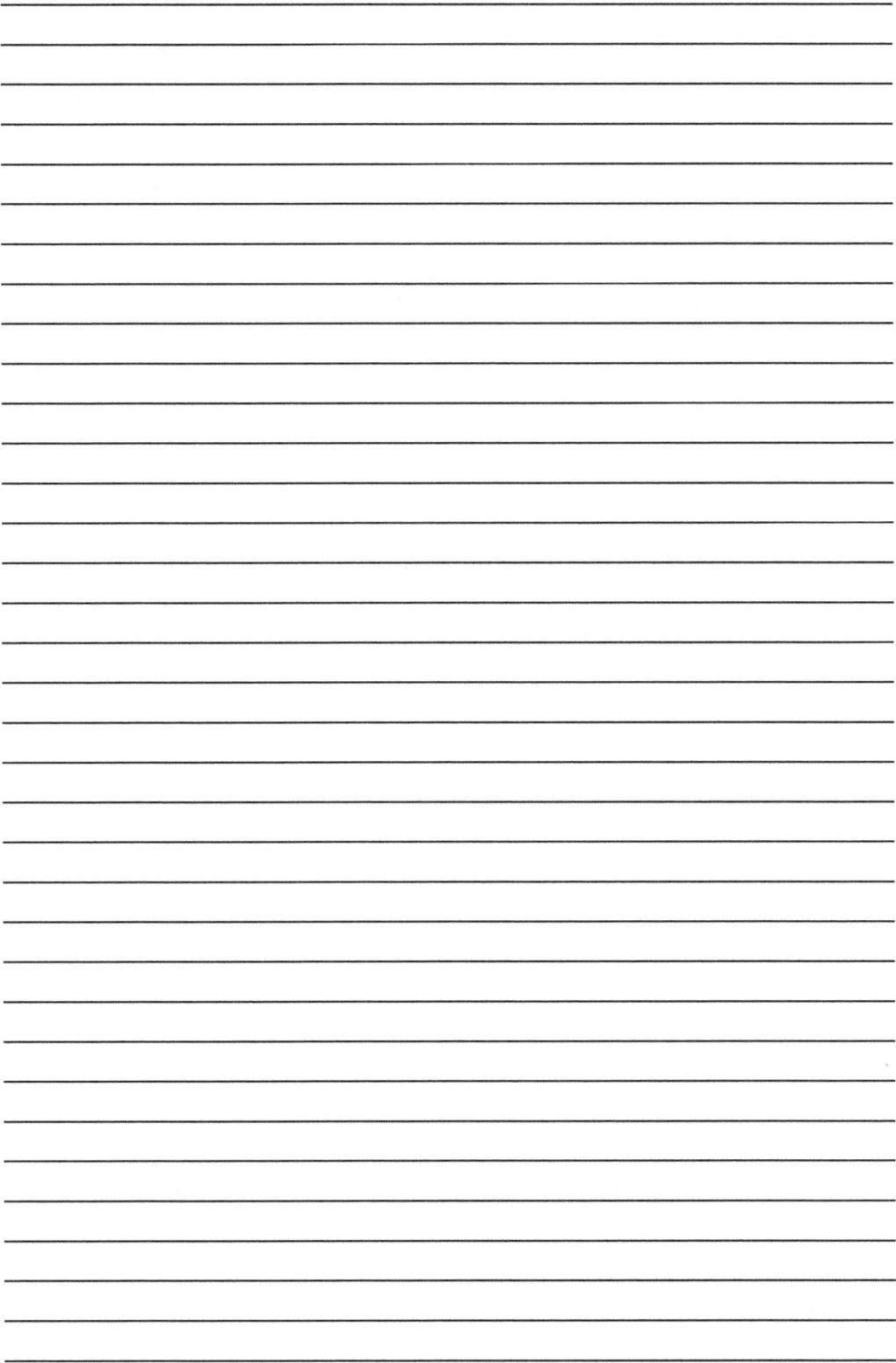

The Good Old Days

In what ways was life different when you were a kid than today? Do you remember your family's first television, telephone, or computer? What things or activities do you wish that people still had or did today? Do you remember family dinners and neighborhood kids playing in the street? What was your favorite meal? What are you glad is no longer around? What things do you miss from when you were little?

_____

_____

_____

_____

_____

_____

_____

_____

_____

_____

_____

_____

_____

_____

_____

_____

_____

_____

_____

_____

_____

_____

_____

_____

_____

Your Earliest Happy Memory

What is your earliest happy memory? Describe that memory. Where were you? Who was with you? What happened? What were the colors, images, and sounds that you recall?

_____

_____

_____

_____

_____

_____

_____

_____

_____

_____

_____

_____

_____

_____

_____

_____

_____

_____

_____

_____

_____

_____

_____

_____

_____

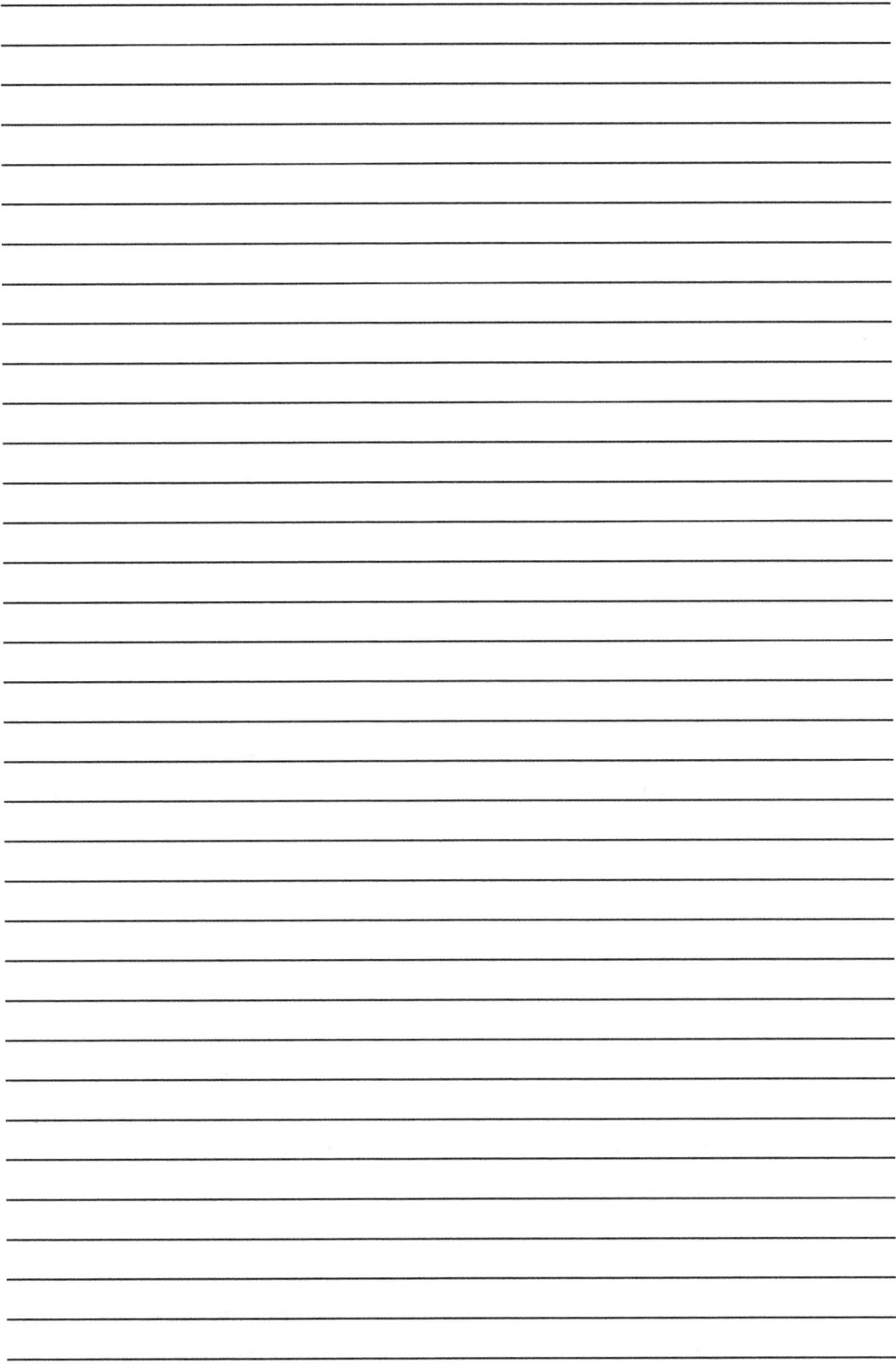

Extraordinary People

Were there people who stood out when you were young? What were they like?
Were there people in your neighborhood who were particularly interesting, creative,
or kind? Record an anecdote about spending time with these people. What did you
learn from them (roller skating, fishing, playing a guitar, baking bread)? What about
them seemed interesting, strange, or fascinating?

_____

_____

_____

_____

_____

_____

_____

_____

_____

_____

_____

_____

_____

_____

_____

_____

_____

_____

_____

_____

_____

_____

_____

_____

_____

_____

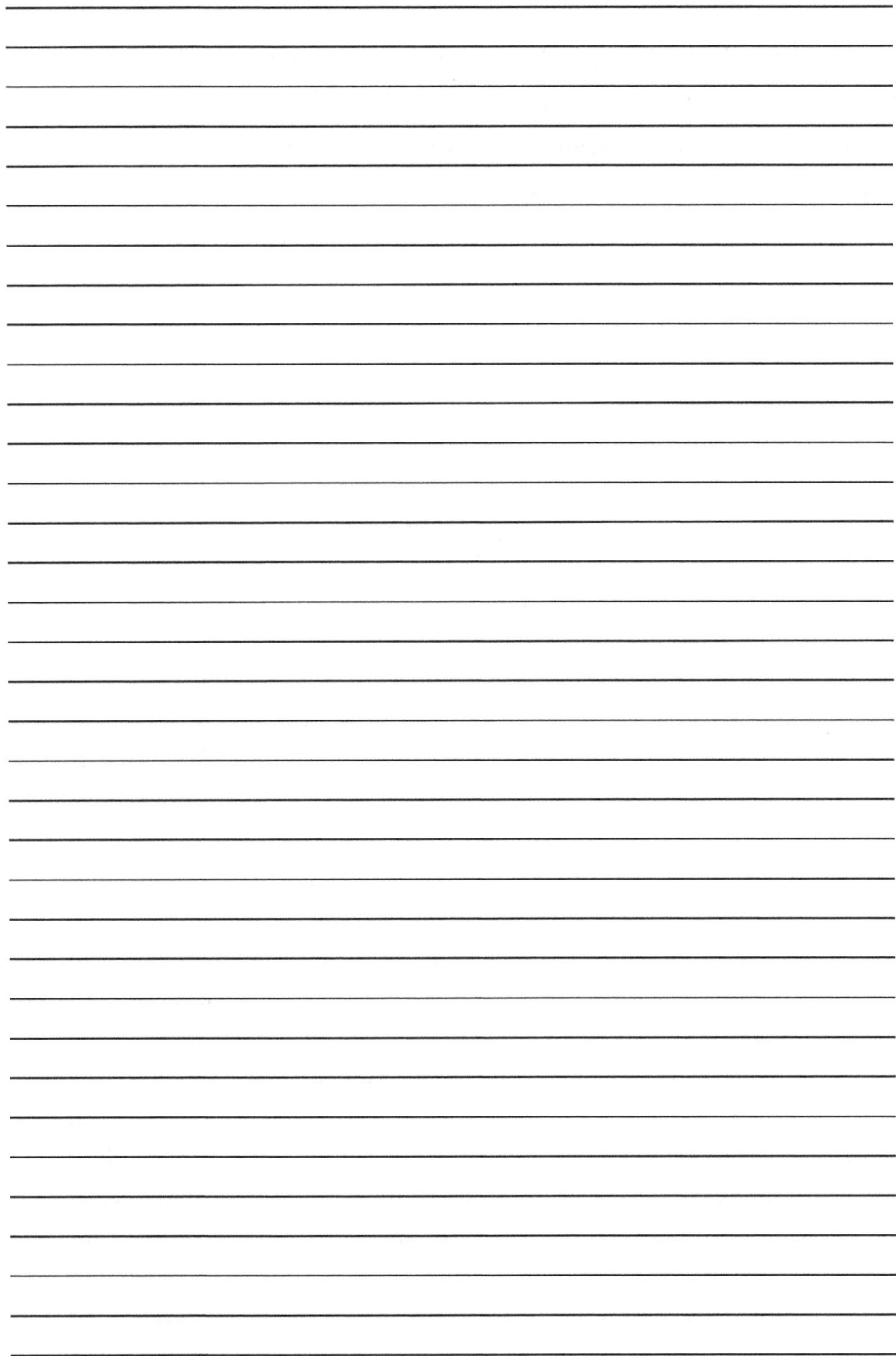

Family Activities

Did your family participate in sports, garden, play board games, or read together? What activities did your family enjoy doing together? What was the family activity you loved the most, and what about it did you love? What family activities annoyed you? What did your parents (or teachers or other people) make you do that drove you crazy? In the end, did you come to appreciate the activities that once were a chore?

_____

_____

_____

_____

_____

_____

_____

_____

_____

_____

_____

_____

_____

_____

_____

_____

_____

_____

_____

_____

_____

_____

_____

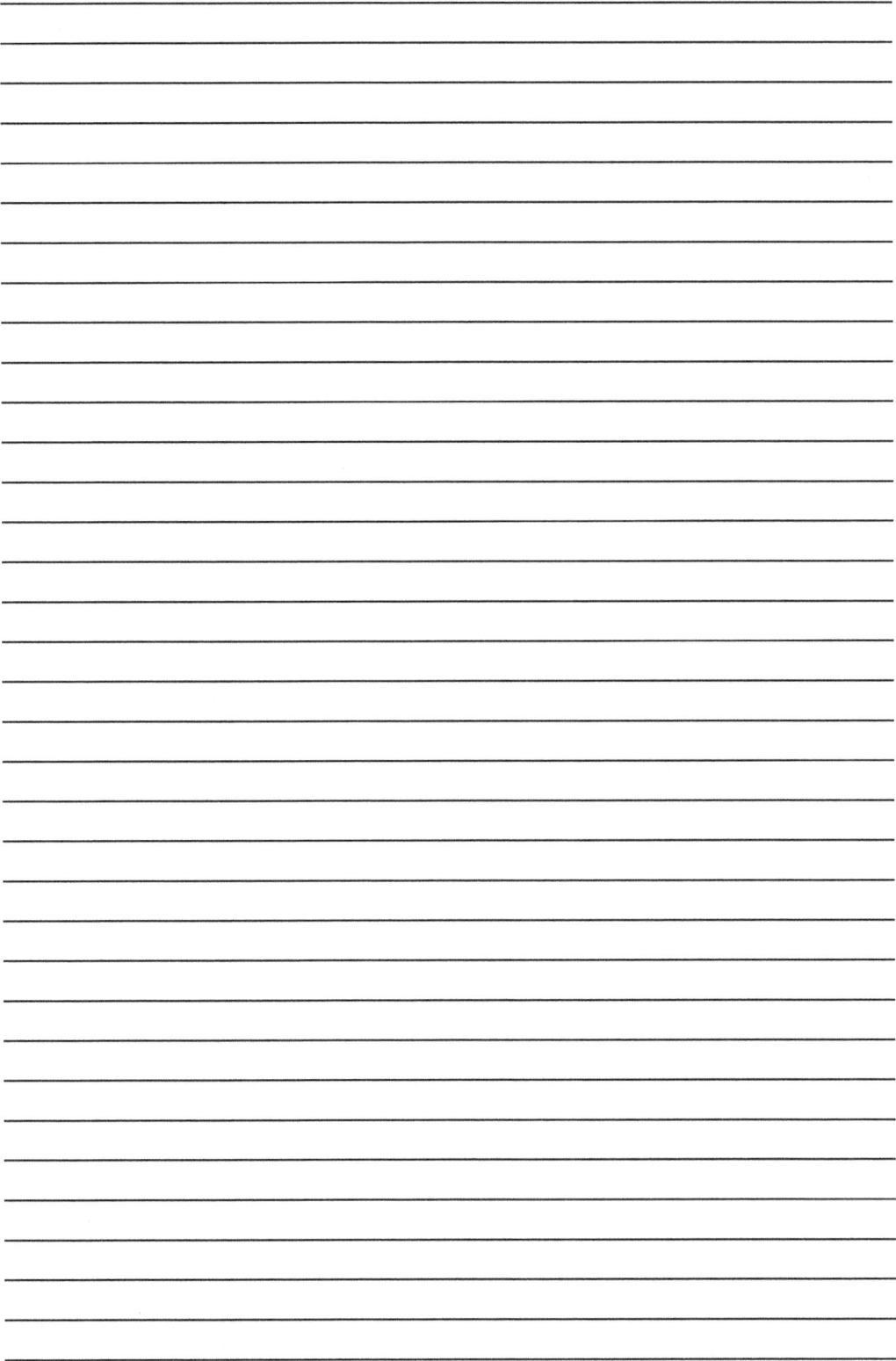

The Whole Family

Attach a photograph or drawing of your family. This might be a snapshot taken at a family reunion, a holiday at home, or a family selfie while on a memorable vacation. Who was in the picture? Where were you and why was it important? Why is this a good representation of your family?

The Lessons of Growing Up

What was it about the activities or events from your childhood that helped make you the person you are today? Did playing baseball teach you about fairness? Did growing up on a farm give you a love of plants or animals? Did you learn to speak another language early on that helped you to travel?

_____

_____

_____

_____

_____

_____

_____

_____

_____

_____

_____

_____

_____

_____

_____

_____

_____

_____

_____

_____

_____

_____

_____

_____

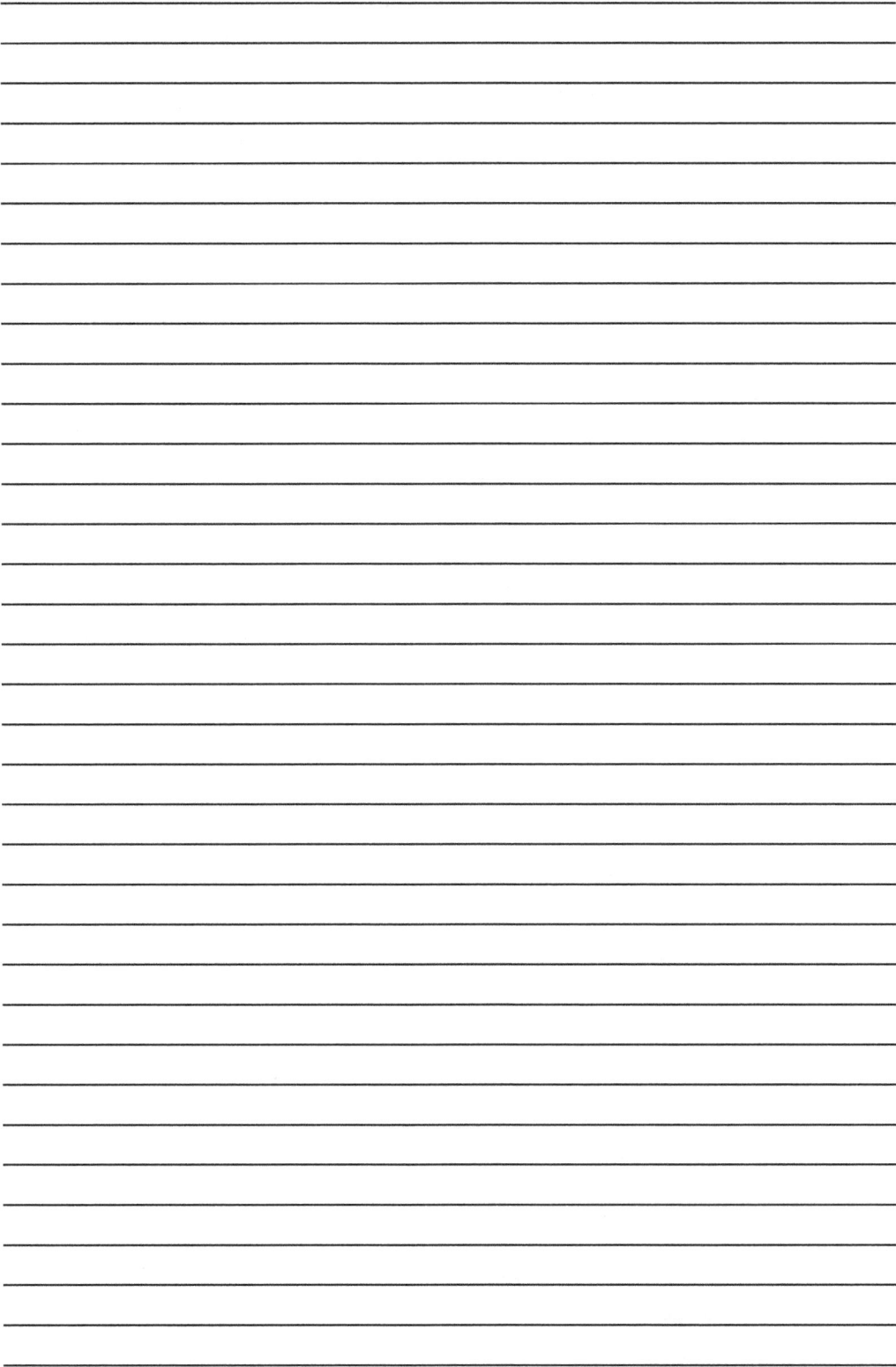

If You Could Experience it Once More

If you had the opportunity, what moment from your past would you return to and relive? What happened in that moment, and why is it worth revisiting? What are the colors, sounds, or tastes that make it stand out? What are the details of that moment that made it extraordinary? What about it comes back into your thoughts over and over again?

_____

_____

_____

_____

_____

_____

_____

_____

_____

_____

_____

_____

_____

_____

_____

_____

_____

_____

_____

_____

_____

_____

_____

_____

_____

_____

Playmates and Friends

Who were your childhood playmates and friends? How did these people influence you (for better or worse)? What did you learn from them? What is an interesting story that you and your friends were involved in when you were young? Did you get into trouble often or did you keep your antics quiet? What advice do you have about friendship and relationships to share with people today?

_____
_____
_____
_____
_____
_____
_____
_____
_____
_____
_____
_____
_____
_____
_____
_____
_____
_____
_____
_____
_____
_____
_____
_____
_____

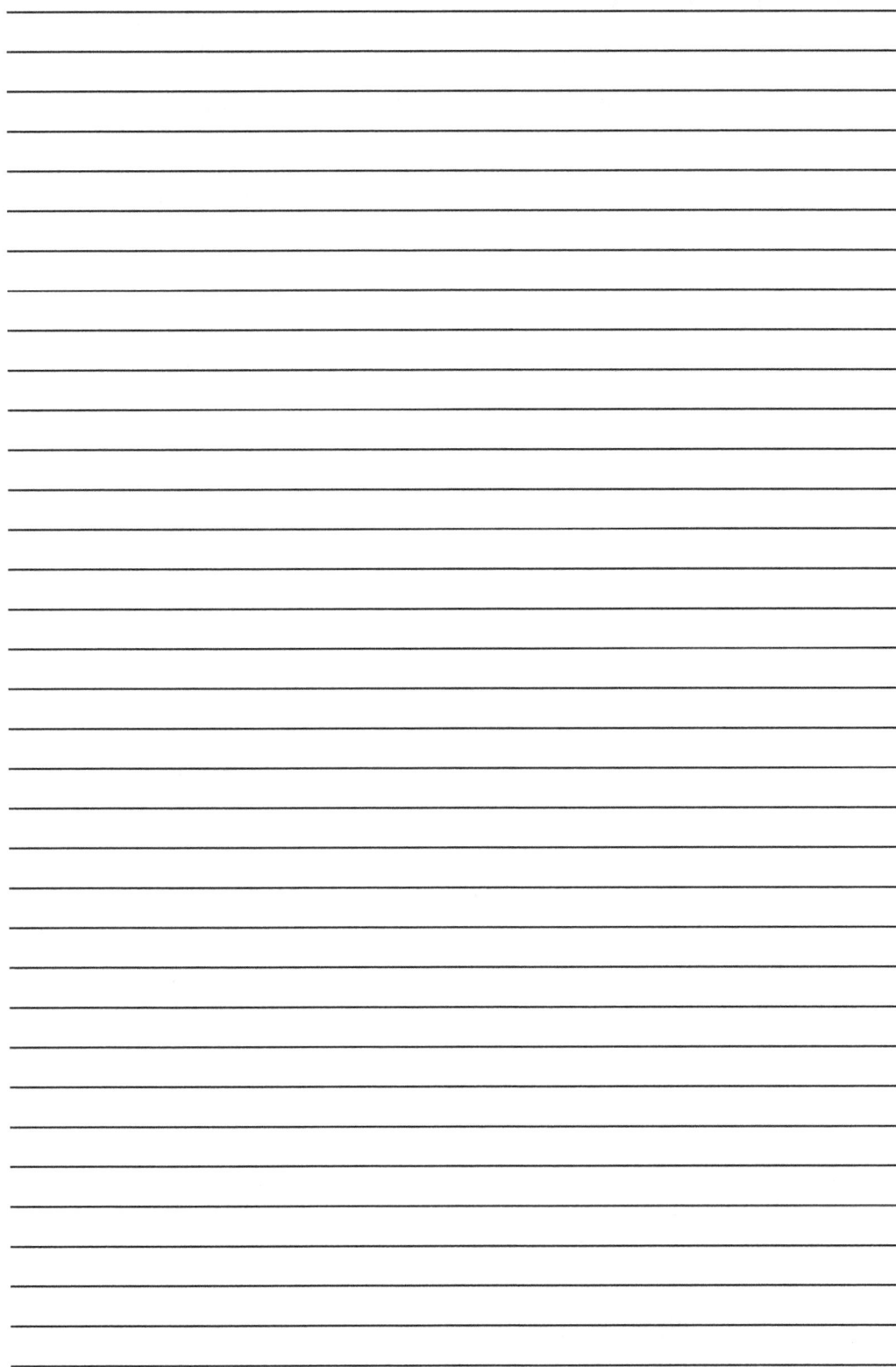

The Education of Life

What schools did you attend? Who were your favorite teachers? What were your favorite subjects in school, and what did you like about them? Do you remember the dusty smell of chalkboards or the musty smell of old libraries? What do you wish that your teachers knew when you were a student? What life lessons did you take away from your education? Did you ever get in trouble? What for? Were you the math kid, the artistic kid, or the theater kid in school?

_____

_____

_____

_____

_____

_____

_____

_____

_____

_____

_____

_____

_____

_____

_____

_____

_____

_____

_____

_____

_____

_____

_____

_____

_____

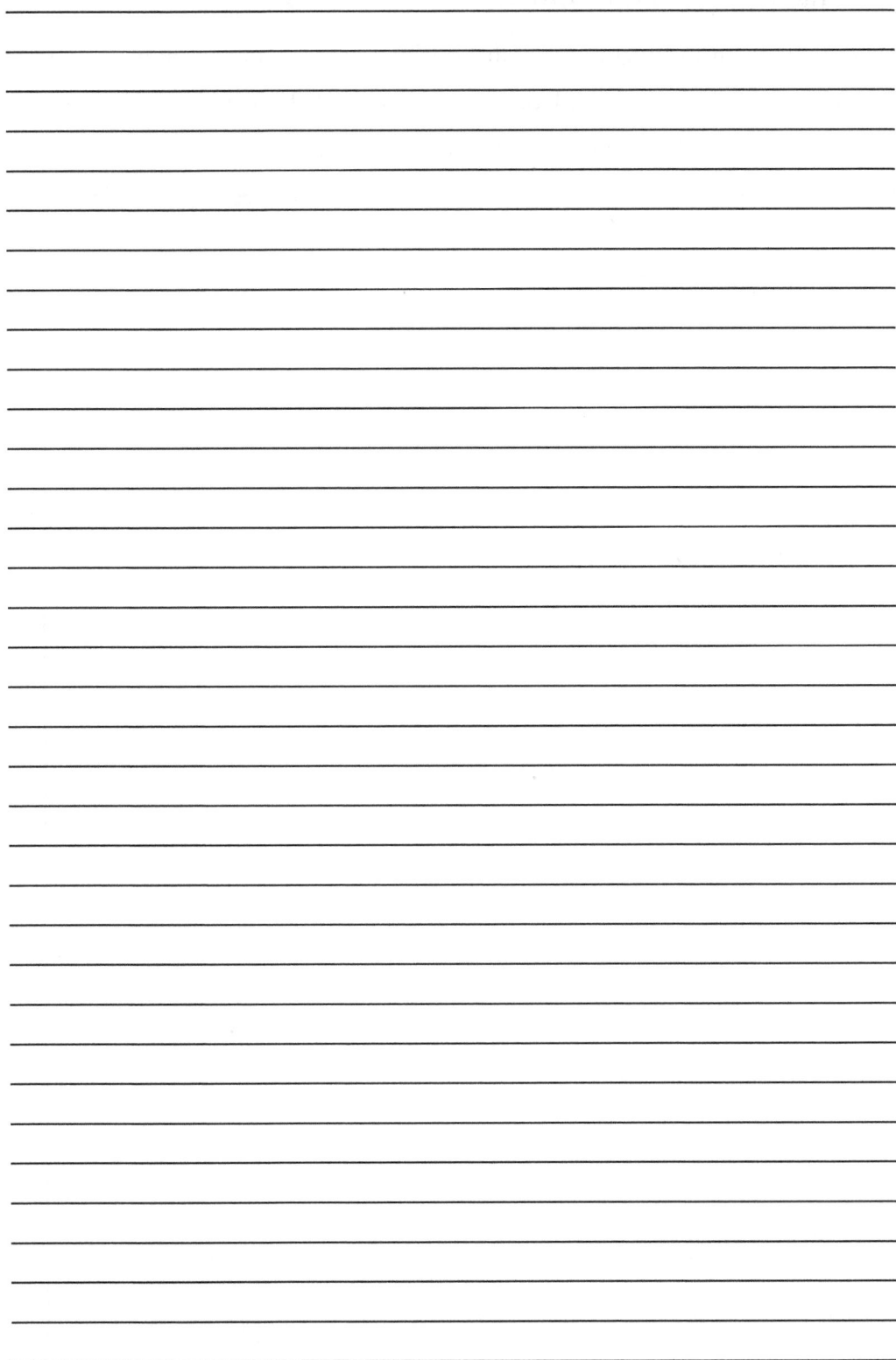

A Moment of Accomplishment

Attach a photo, memento, or artifact that celebrates one of your accomplishments. This might be a ribbon, an award, or a letter of acknowledgment. It may be a photo of you graduating, celebrating a special moment, or you with a group of friends or colleagues enjoying your victory together. Below explain the significance of this celebration and its impact on you.

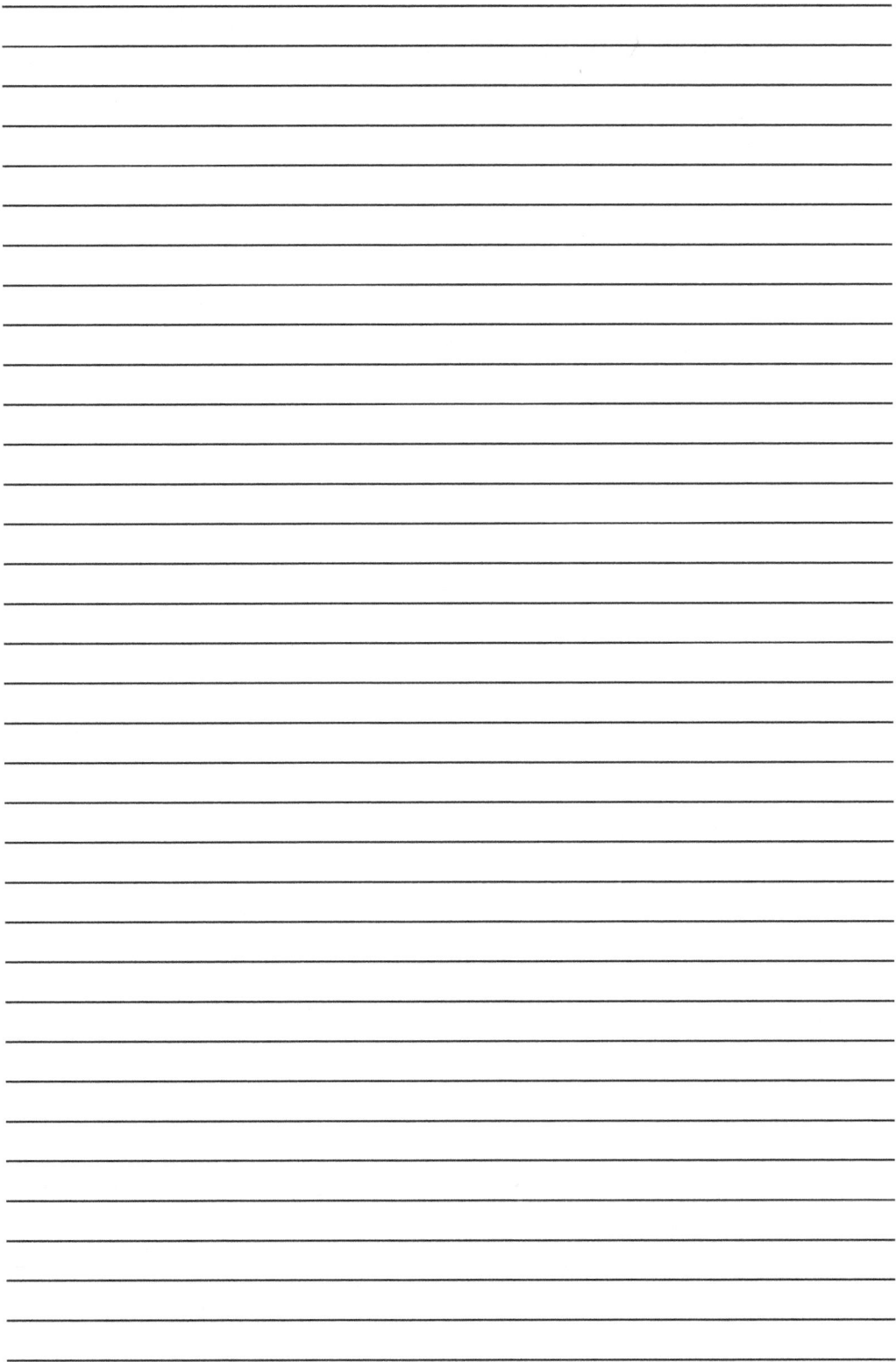

If You Could Learn Anew

If you could go back and focus your education in a different way, how might you change it? What about your education taught you the lessons you needed to accomplish your personal or professional goals? What advice do you have for students?

_____

_____

_____

_____

_____

_____

_____

_____

_____

_____

_____

_____

_____

_____

_____

_____

_____

_____

_____

_____

_____

_____

_____

_____

_____

_____

_____

_____

Religion and Spirituality

Did you ever belong to a church or a religion? Why was that important to you, and if you are still involved, why do you participate? What advice about religion or spirituality or about being tolerant or open to religion do you have to share?

_____

_____

_____

_____

_____

_____

_____

_____

_____

_____

_____

_____

_____

_____

_____

_____

_____

_____

_____

_____

_____

_____

_____

_____

_____

_____

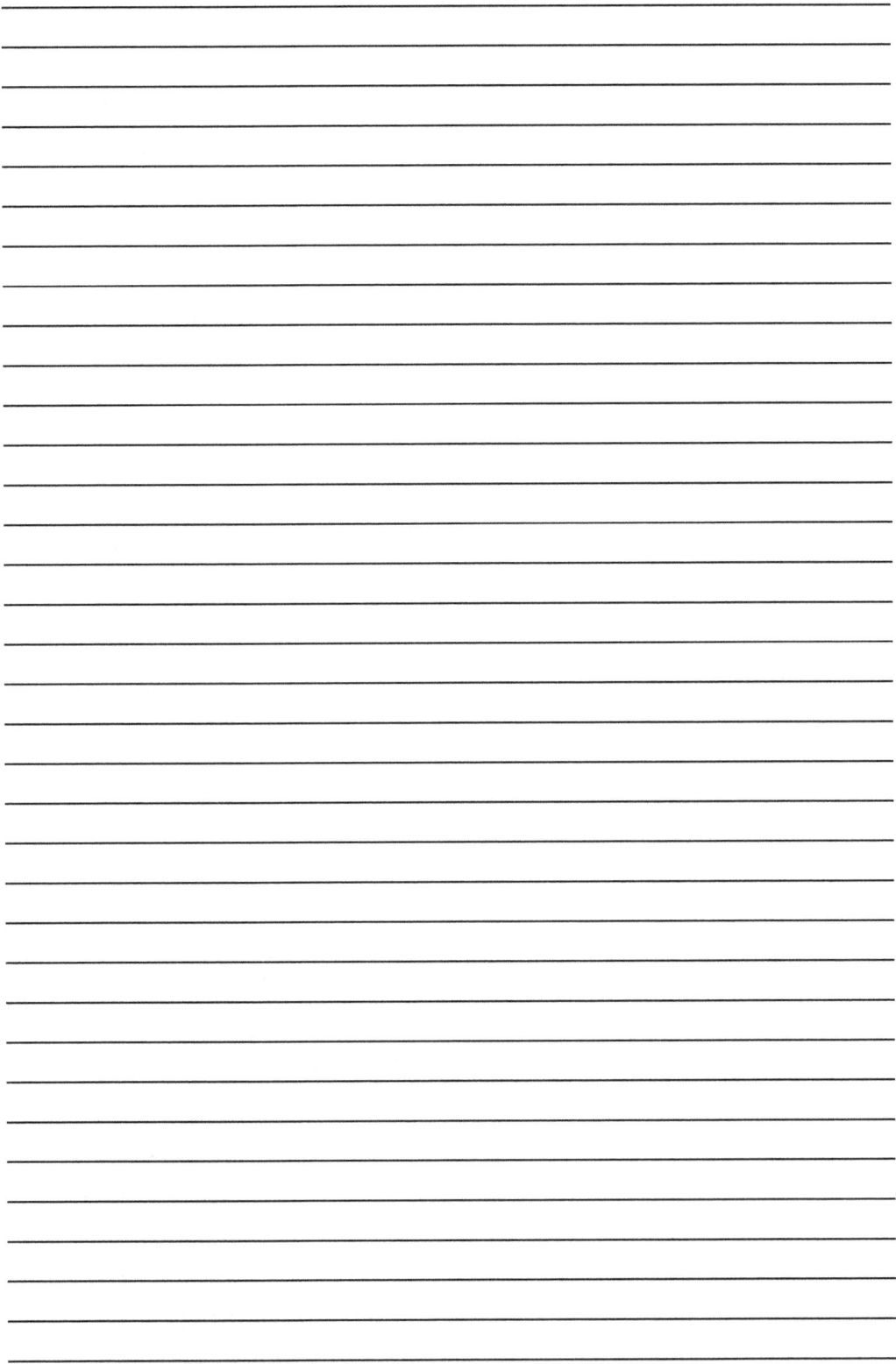

The 10 Books You Would Take

If you were left on a desert island for a year with ten books of your choice, what would they be? Why would you choose those books for your island stay? What about those books would keep you interested, informed, and entertained for the year? Would you recommend these books to others? Why or why not? If not books, what would you want to be left with (recipes, movies, art works)?

_____

_____

_____

_____

_____

_____

_____

_____

_____

_____

_____

_____

_____

_____

_____

_____

_____

_____

_____

_____

_____

_____

_____

_____

_____

_____

_____

_____

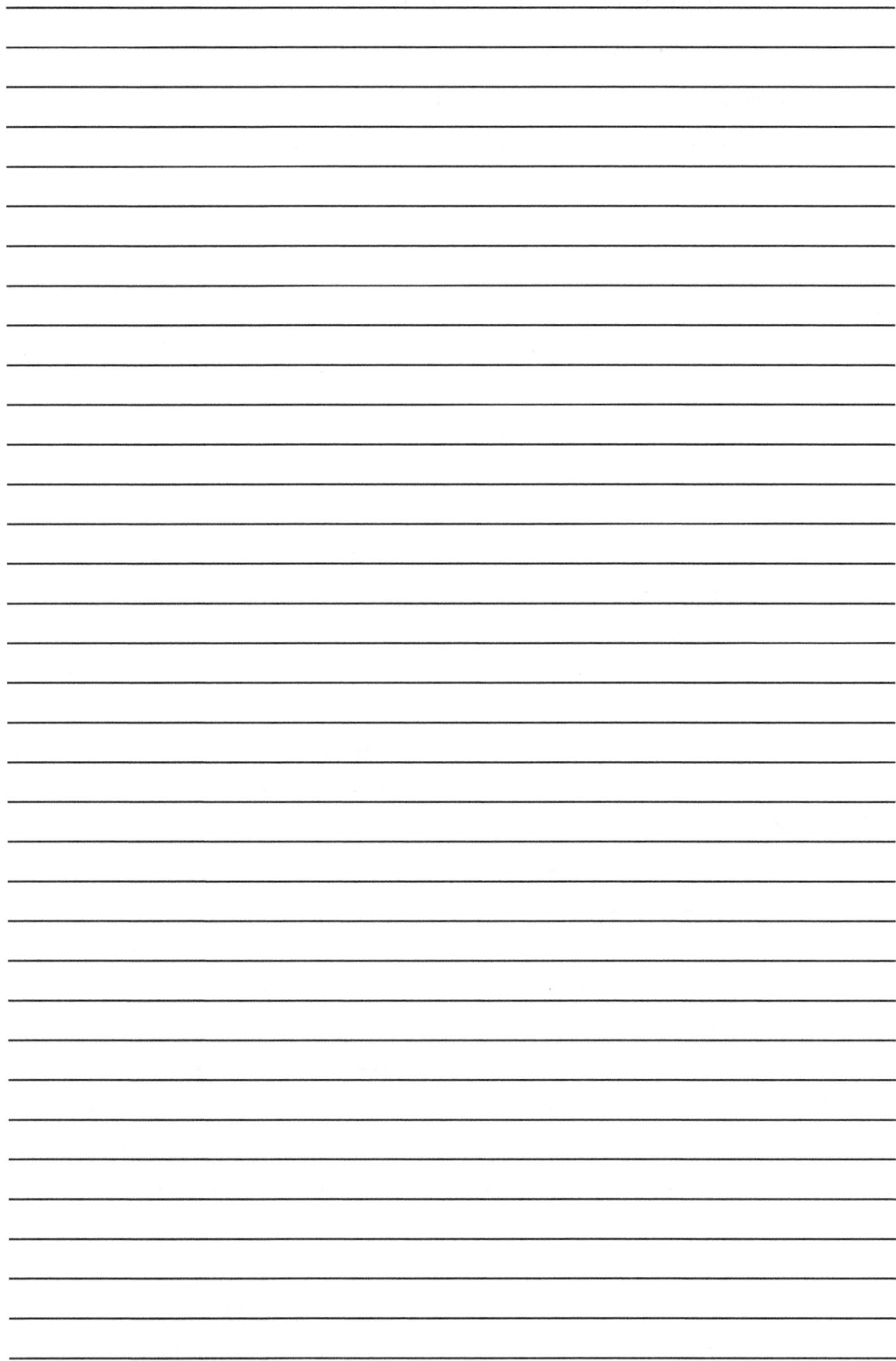

You'll Always Remember Your First Love

Who was your first love? When was your first kiss? When was your first heartbreak? Your first date? Did you ever go on a double date with friends? What was dating like when you were young? What did you learn about love by allowing yourself to be vulnerable?

_____

_____

_____

_____

_____

_____

_____

_____

_____

_____

_____

_____

_____

_____

_____

_____

_____

_____

_____

_____

_____

_____

_____

_____

_____

_____

_____

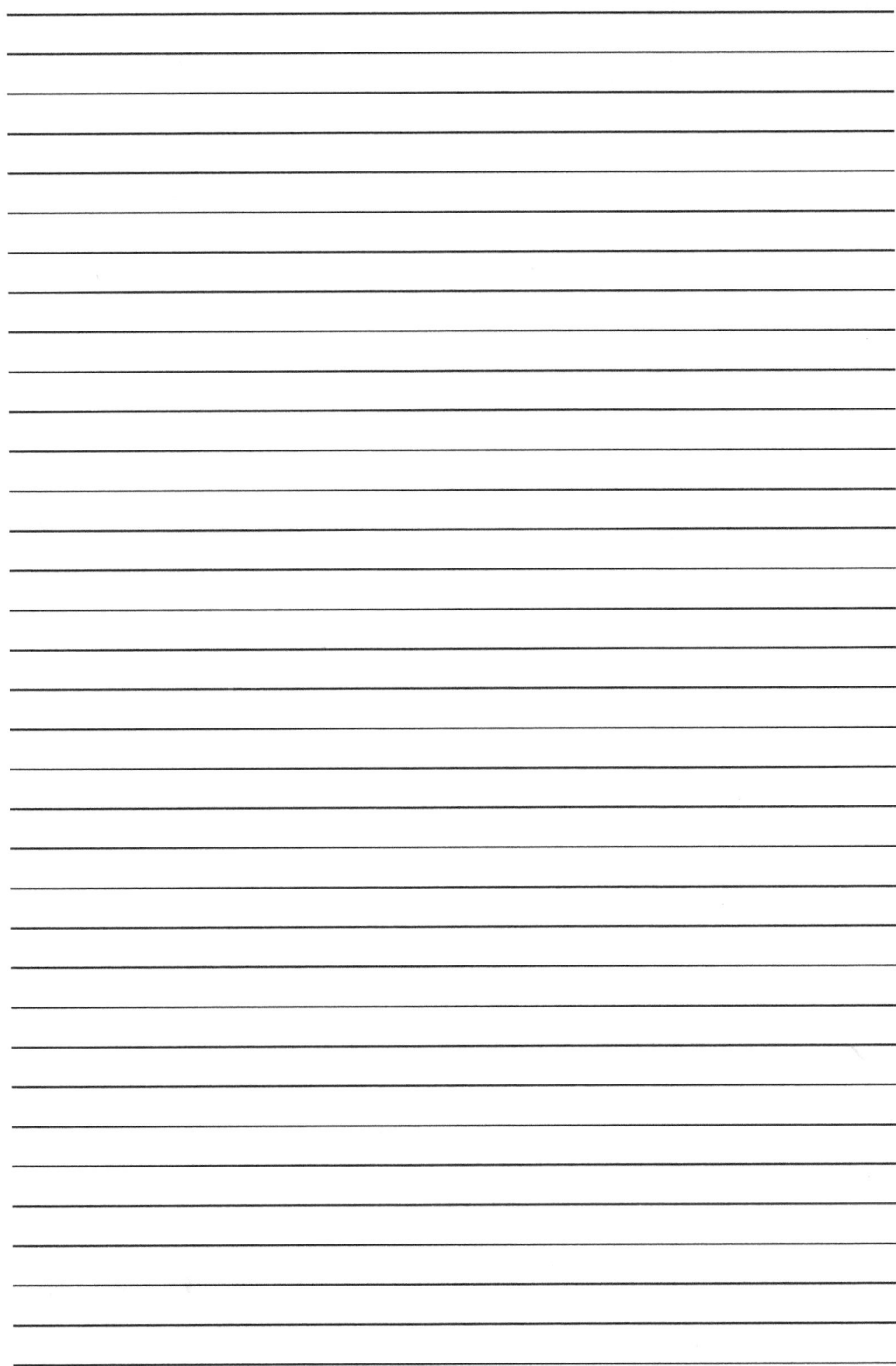

The Image of Love

Attach a picture of what love means to you. Perhaps you have a photo of a favored pet. Maybe you have a picture of yourself with a group of friends. Or perhaps attach your wedding picture, an image of you with your best friend, or a drawing or piece of art from a person you love. Explain the significance of this piece below.

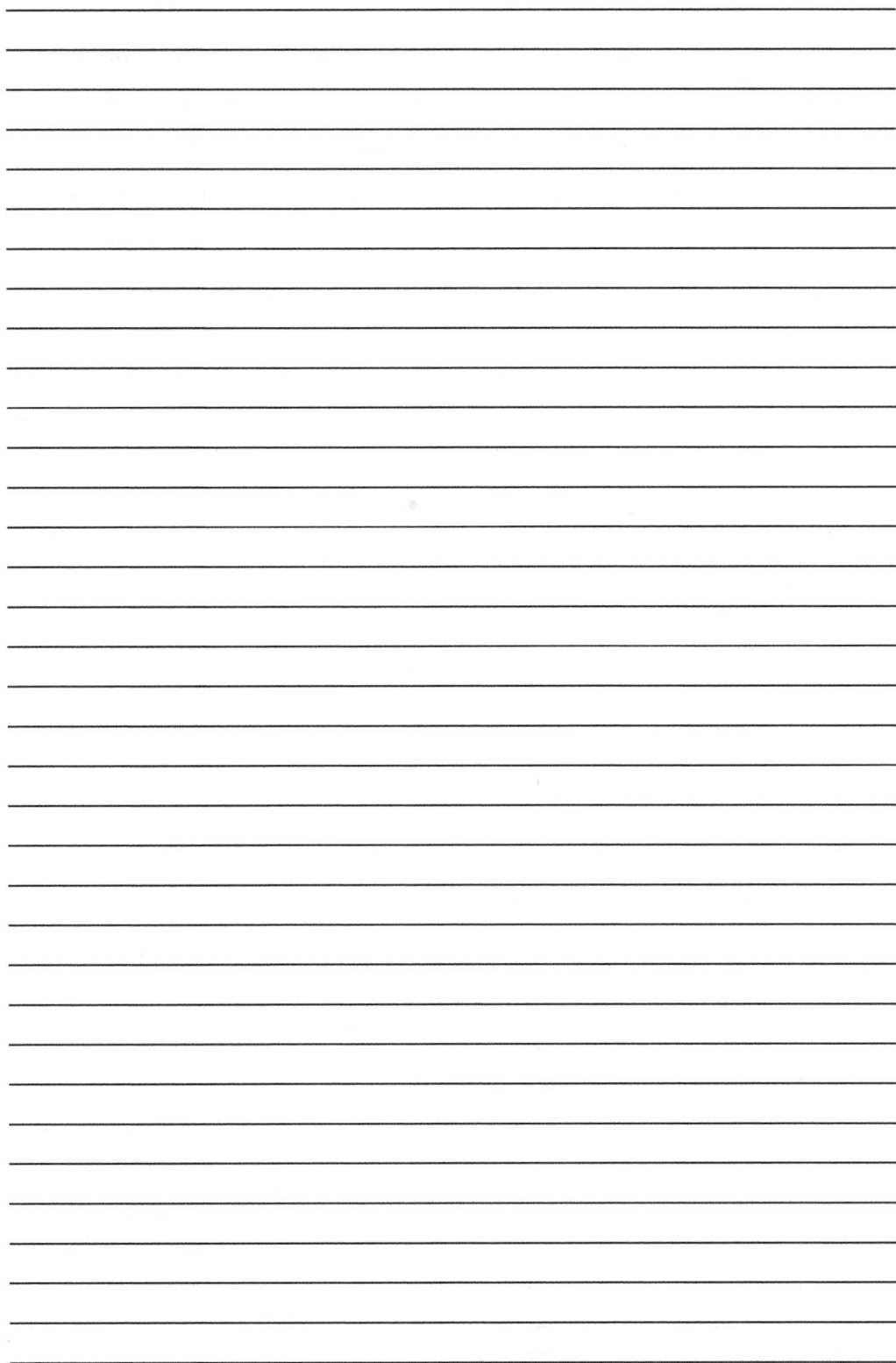

Your Teen Years

What were you like as a teenager? Did you like hot rods, line dancing, or making abstract art? How would you describe your style when you were a young adult? Were you popular or focused on just a small group of friends? What were the fads during your teen years?   What were the best films and the best musicians of your young adult years? What song lyrics spoke to you and what was your favorite song from that time period? Did you turn to music as a stress reliever?

_____

_____

_____

_____

_____

_____

_____

_____

_____

_____

_____

_____

_____

_____

_____

_____

_____

_____

_____

_____

_____

_____

_____

_____

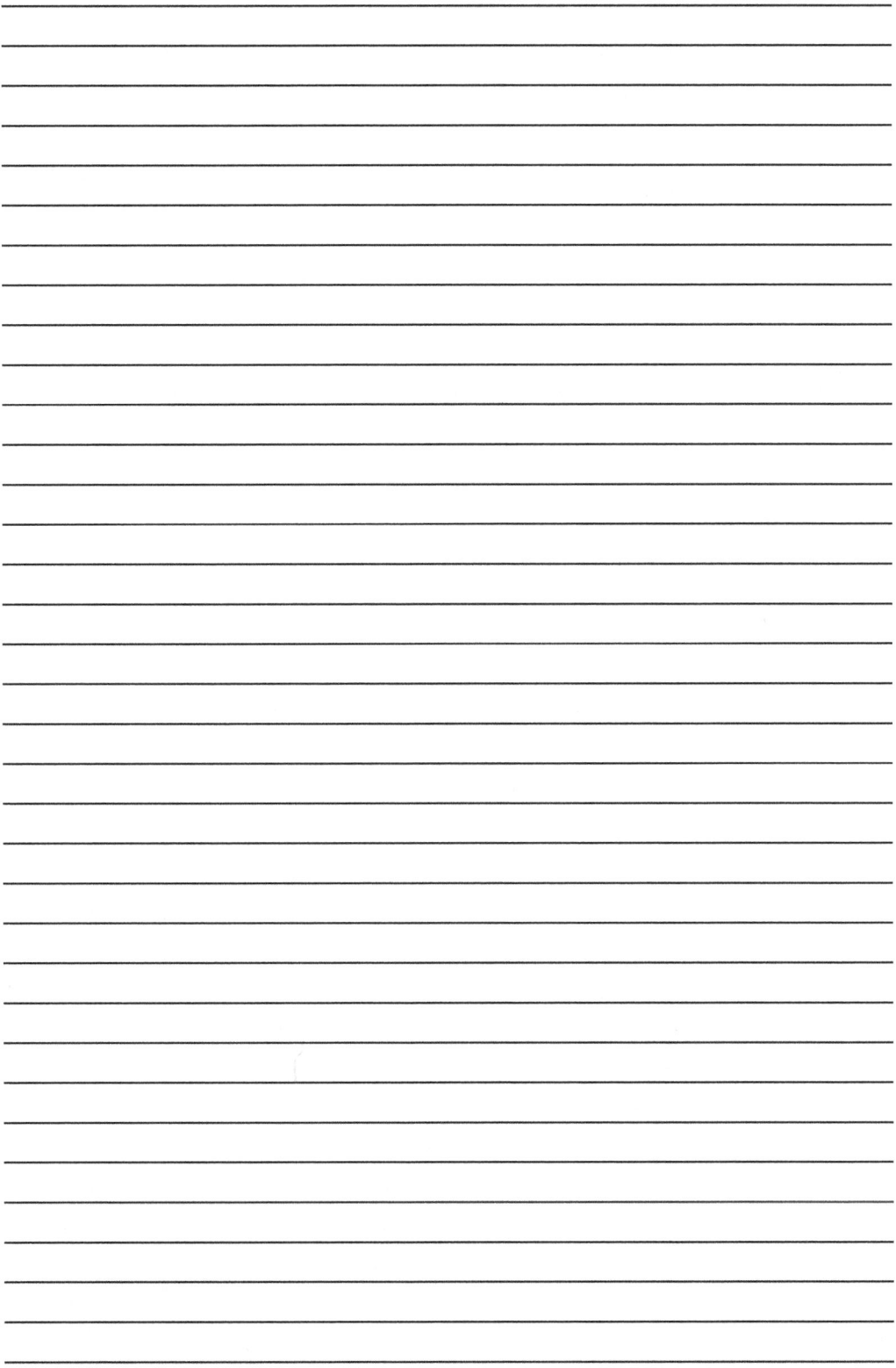

Almost an Adult

Were your young adult years a time to look back on with fondness and happy memories or were those years best left in the past? What did you learn about life by being a young adult? What advice would you give to young people today? Share a story of a formative event from those years.

_____

_____

_____

_____

_____

_____

_____

_____

_____

_____

_____

_____

_____

_____

_____

_____

_____

_____

_____

_____

_____

_____

_____

_____

_____

_____

_____

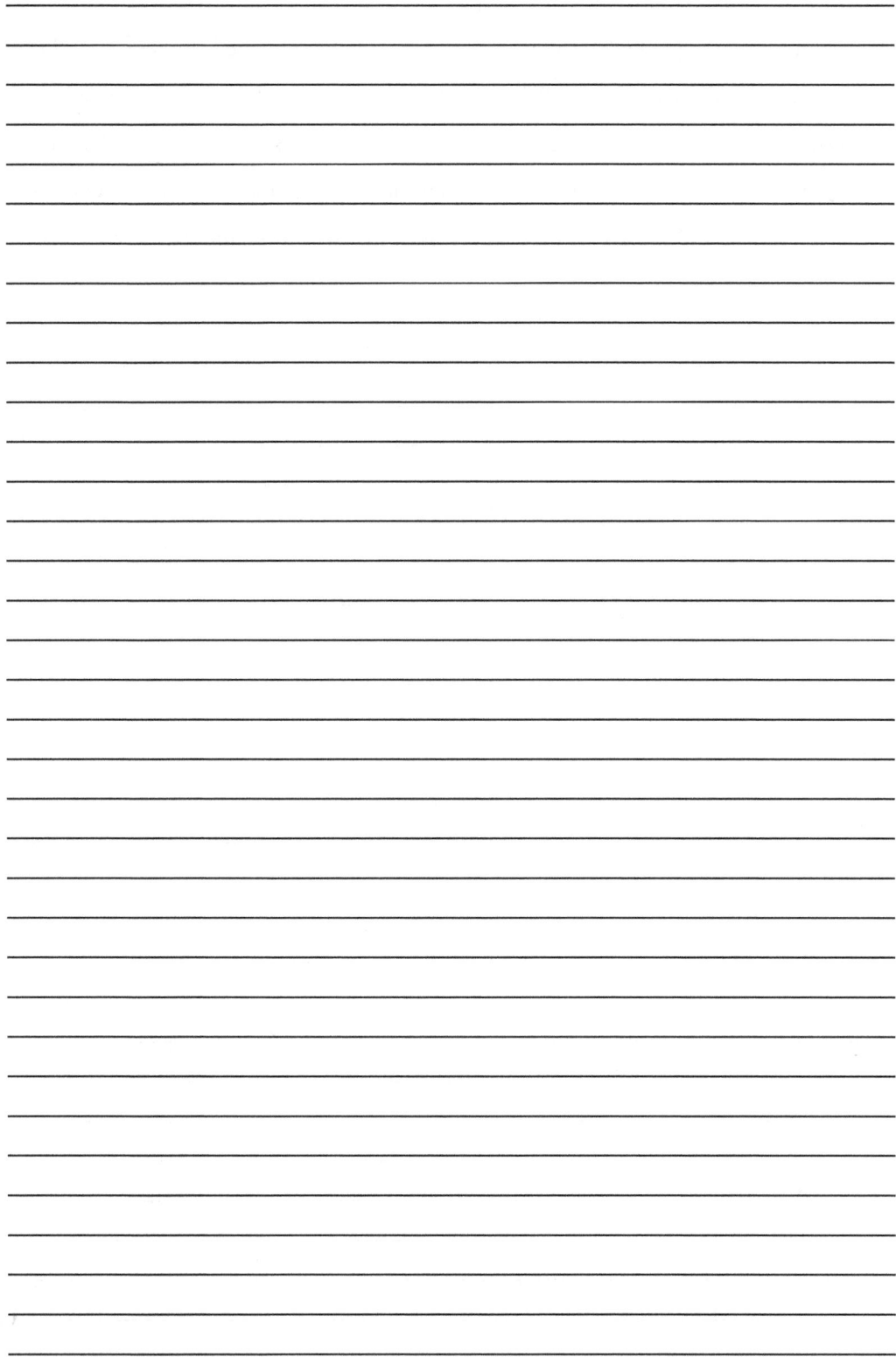

The Events that Impacted You

The last century was packed with exceptional events that changed the world, and the world changed on a yearly basis. Where were you when you heard about President Kennedy's assassination? What did you think of the Beatles? How did the Vietnam War or the turmoil at home affect you? What did your friends think about world events like the Civil Rights, Feminist, and Environmental movements? What events impacted you the most?

_____
_____
_____
_____
_____
_____
_____
_____
_____
_____
_____
_____
_____
_____
_____
_____
_____
_____
_____
_____
_____
_____
_____

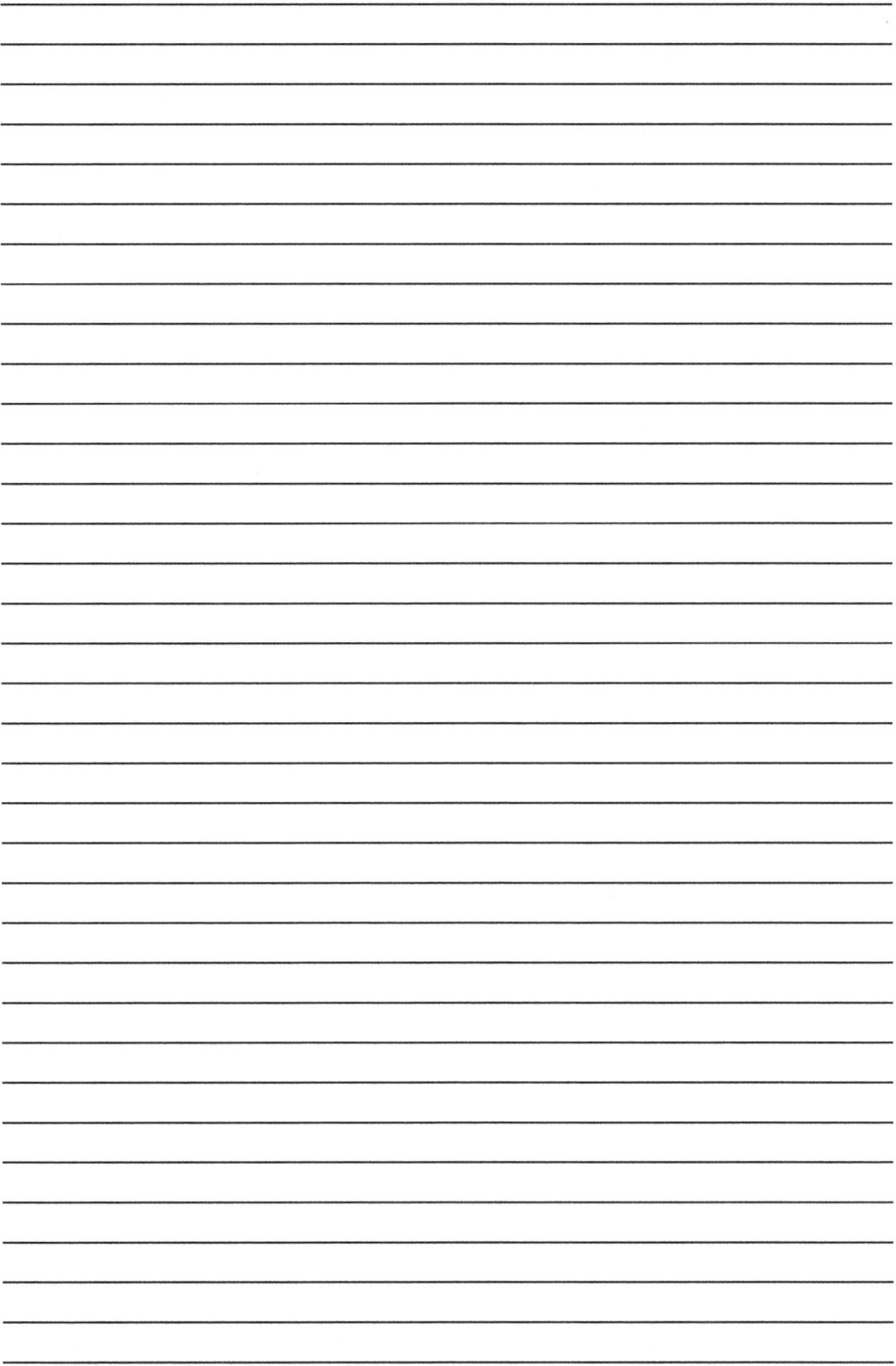

Friends are the Family we Choose

What were your friendships and relationships like when you were a young adult? Are you still in contact with people from your high school or college years? What worked well about relationships from those years and what could have been better? How did your early years prepare you for adulthood? If you could go back and do it all over again, would you change anything about those years? Who was your best friend when you were 10? When you were 20? When you were 30?

_____

_____

_____

_____

_____

_____

_____

_____

_____

_____

_____

_____

_____

_____

_____

_____

_____

_____

_____

_____

_____

_____

_____

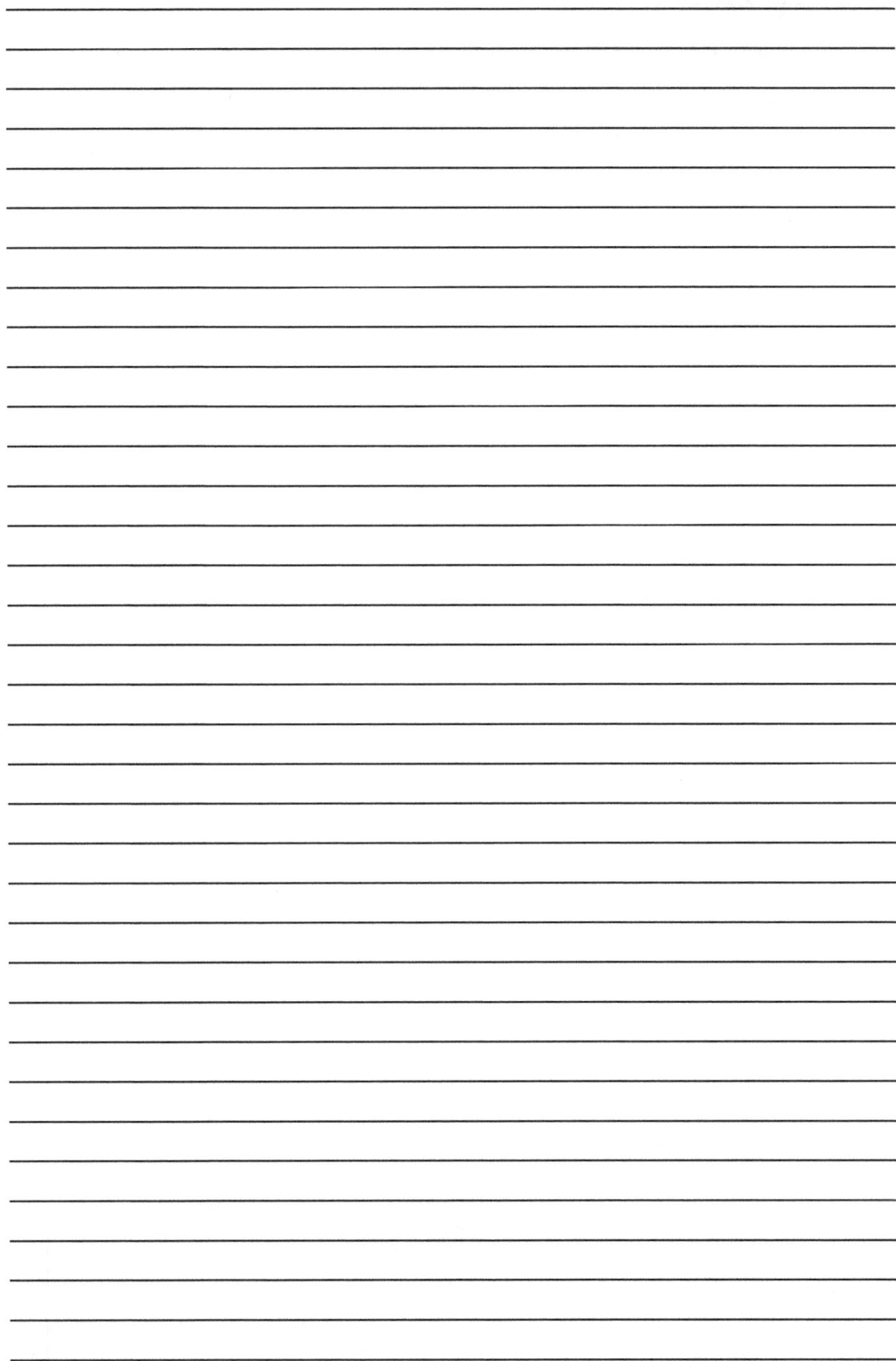

Keep Your Friends Close

Attach an image of friendship. Perhaps you will choose an image of a long-lost friend you once held dear. Maybe your photo is of a team or group who stuck together through thick and thin. Or you may choose a mentor, a colleague or a hero. Explain the importance of the image and the connection to your life.

Love and Marriage

If you married, when did you meet your partner? How and where did you meet? What was your first date? When did you fall in love? How long did you wait to marry? What was valuable about your marriage and what elements of it do you look back on with fondness? If you married multiple times, what about each of those relationships was treasured? What memories do you cherish most?

_____

_____

_____

_____

_____

_____

_____

_____

_____

_____

_____

_____

_____

_____

_____

_____

_____

_____

_____

_____

_____

_____

_____

_____

_____

_____

_____

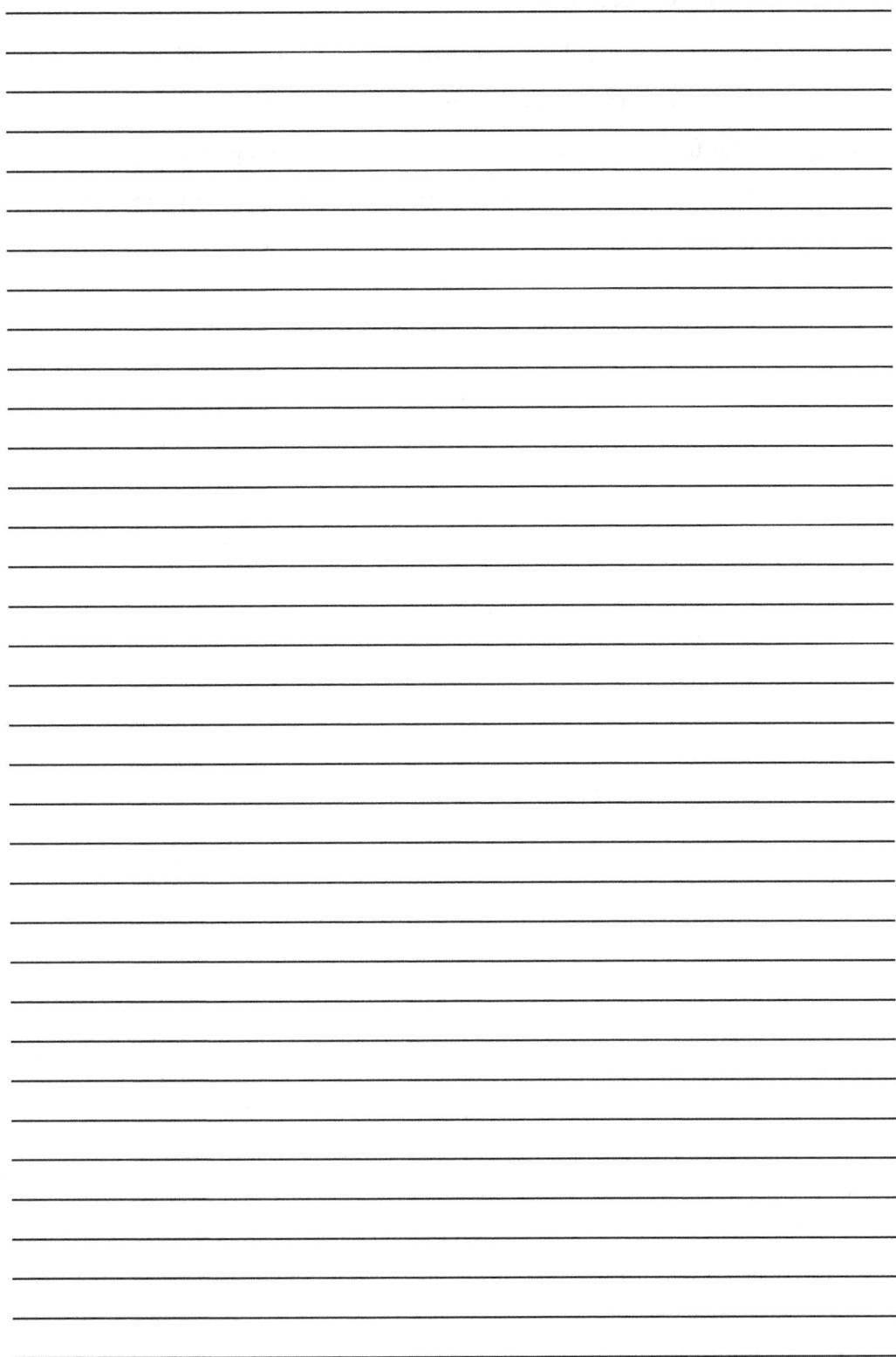

Heart, Head, or Pocketbook

If you did not marry, or married and pursued a career, what goals did you pursue (a business, an art, travel, caring for family, etc.)? What was your first full-time job? How big was your first paycheck? What accomplishments are you most proud of? What advice about life choices can you pass onto young people? Is it best to follow your heart, your head, or your pocketbook? Why?

_____

_____

_____

_____

_____

_____

_____

_____

_____

_____

_____

_____

_____

_____

_____

_____

_____

_____

_____

_____

_____

_____

_____

_____

The Big Day

If you married, describe the details of your wedding. What did you wear? What was the music? Did you have dinner, cake, or champagne? How about a honeymoon? What did you enjoy about your wedding, and what now makes you cringe a little bit? What suggestions do you have about planning or attending large events?

_____

_____

_____

_____

_____

_____

_____

_____

_____

_____

_____

_____

_____

_____

_____

_____

_____

_____

_____

_____

_____

_____

_____

_____

_____

_____

_____

Accomplishments worth Celebration

Did you have different types of celebrations in your adult years? Perhaps a graduation, an acceptance of an award, the publishing of a book, employee of the month, or some other moment when your life changed or your accomplishments were acknowledged?

_____

_____

_____

_____

_____

_____

_____

_____

_____

_____

_____

_____

_____

_____

_____

_____

_____

_____

_____

_____

_____

_____

_____

_____

_____

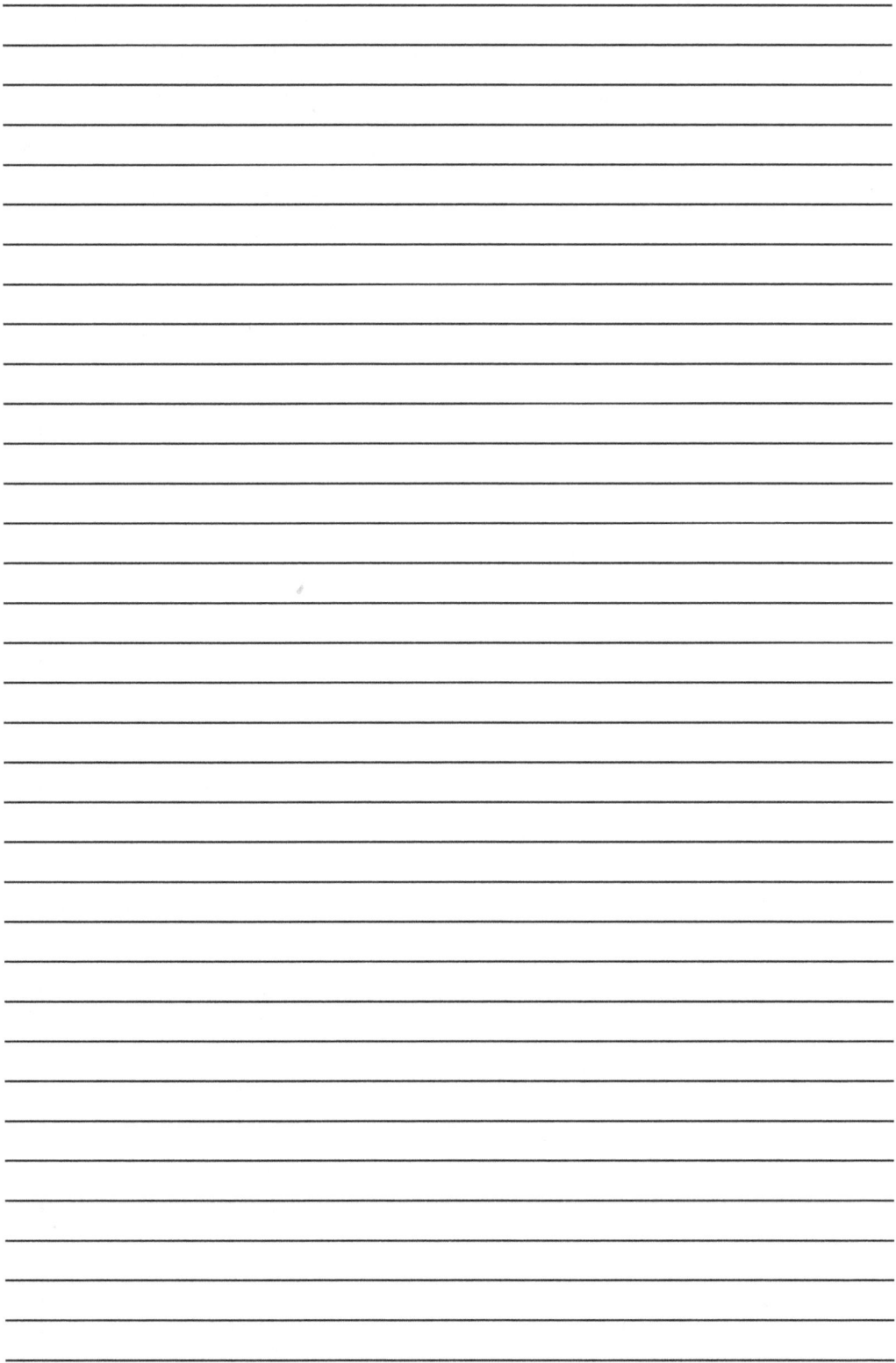

Admiration and Gratitude

Attach an image of something or someone you admire or are grateful for. You may choose a place in nature, a home, a travel destination that changed you. Perhaps an event, time period, or experience changed the path of your life in some way. Maybe a person came into your life at just the right time. Include an image, a drawing, or a keepsake of that something or someone for which you hold admiration and gratitude. Explain the image below.

The Skills to Succeed

Did you attend trade school, college, or learn a skill through an internship or apprenticeship? How did you learn the skills needed to succeed as an adult? What are the skills you value and have used the most? What skills did you wish you mastered earlier in life? If you could write a letter to your younger self and suggest working harder to learn something, what would that be?

_____

_____

_____

_____

_____

_____

_____

_____

_____

_____

_____

_____

_____

_____

_____

_____

_____

_____

_____

_____

_____

_____

_____

_____

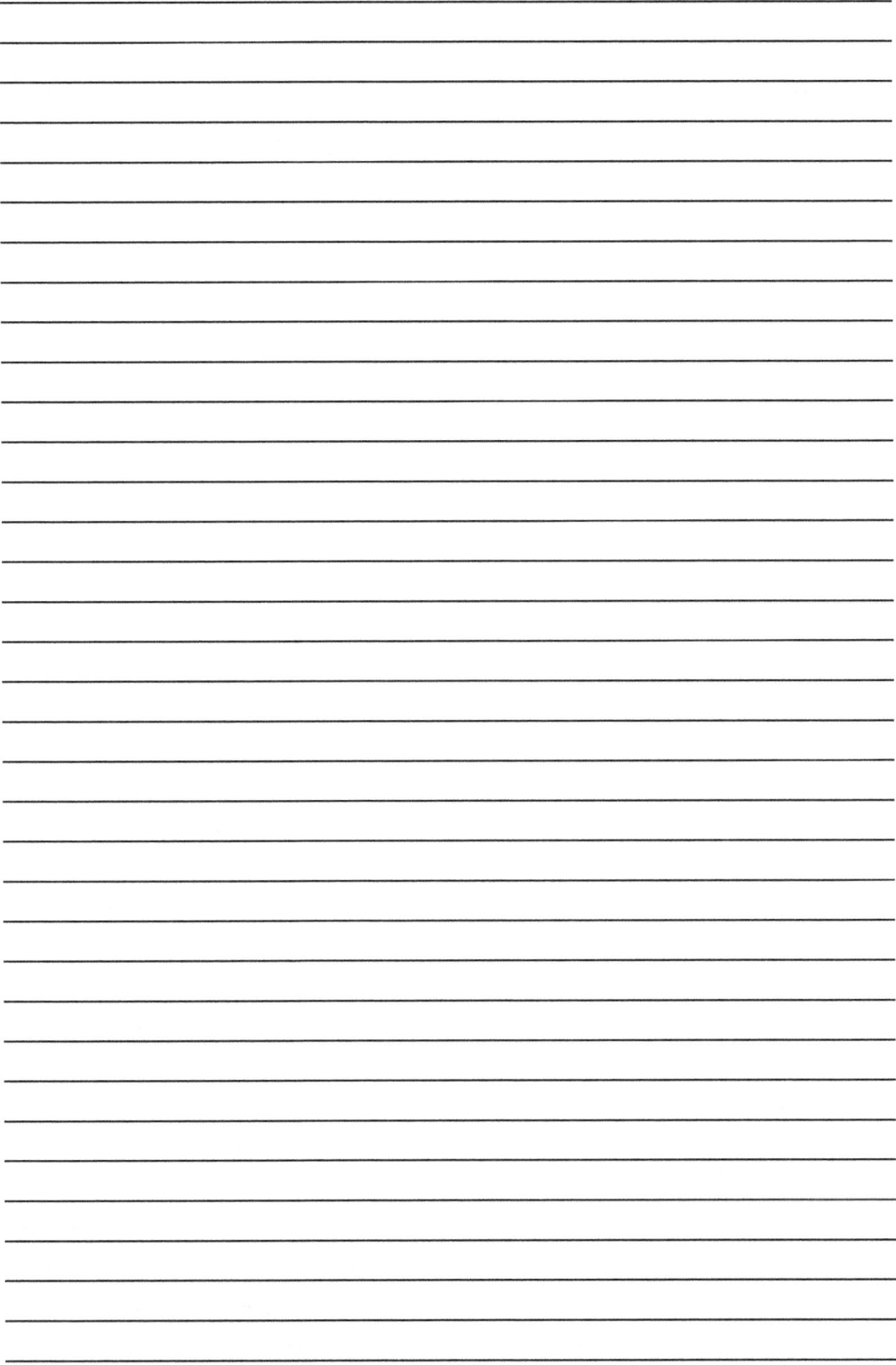

Children

Do you have children? If so, what are their names and birthdays? What are some special memories you have of your children? What did you learn about yourself by raising children and how did you grow as a person during those years? What are your favorite memories with your children?

_____

_____

_____

_____

_____

_____

_____

_____

_____

_____

_____

_____

_____

_____

_____

_____

_____

_____

_____

_____

_____

_____

_____

_____

_____

_____

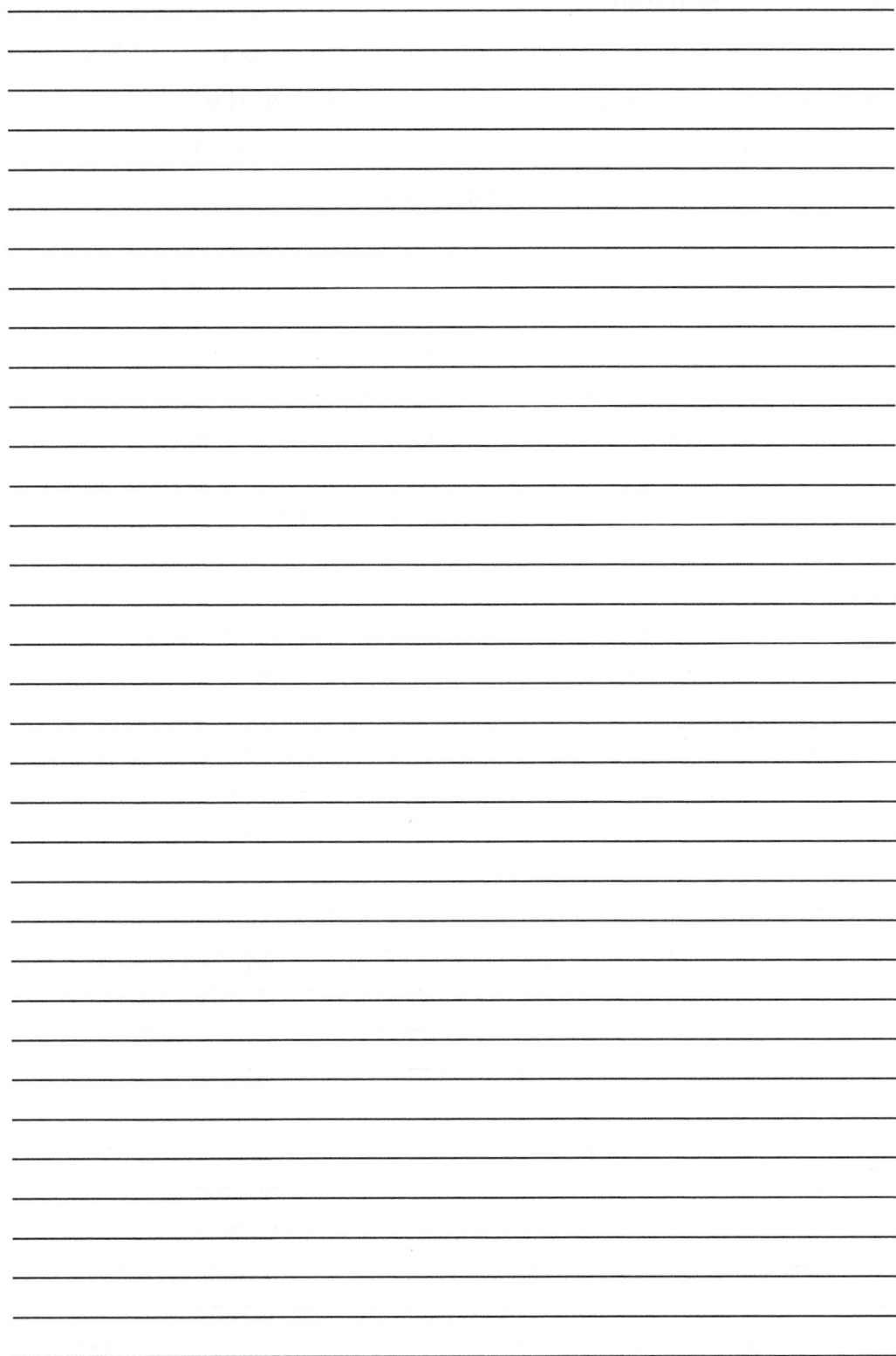

That Special Someone

Do you have pets, friends, or family members who are important to you? What are some special memories you have of them? When did you feel closest to them? What major events did you experience together? How do you most enjoy spending time with them (golf, baking, walking along the beach)?

_____

_____

_____

_____

_____

_____

_____

_____

_____

_____

_____

_____

_____

_____

_____

_____

_____

_____

_____

_____

_____

_____

_____

_____

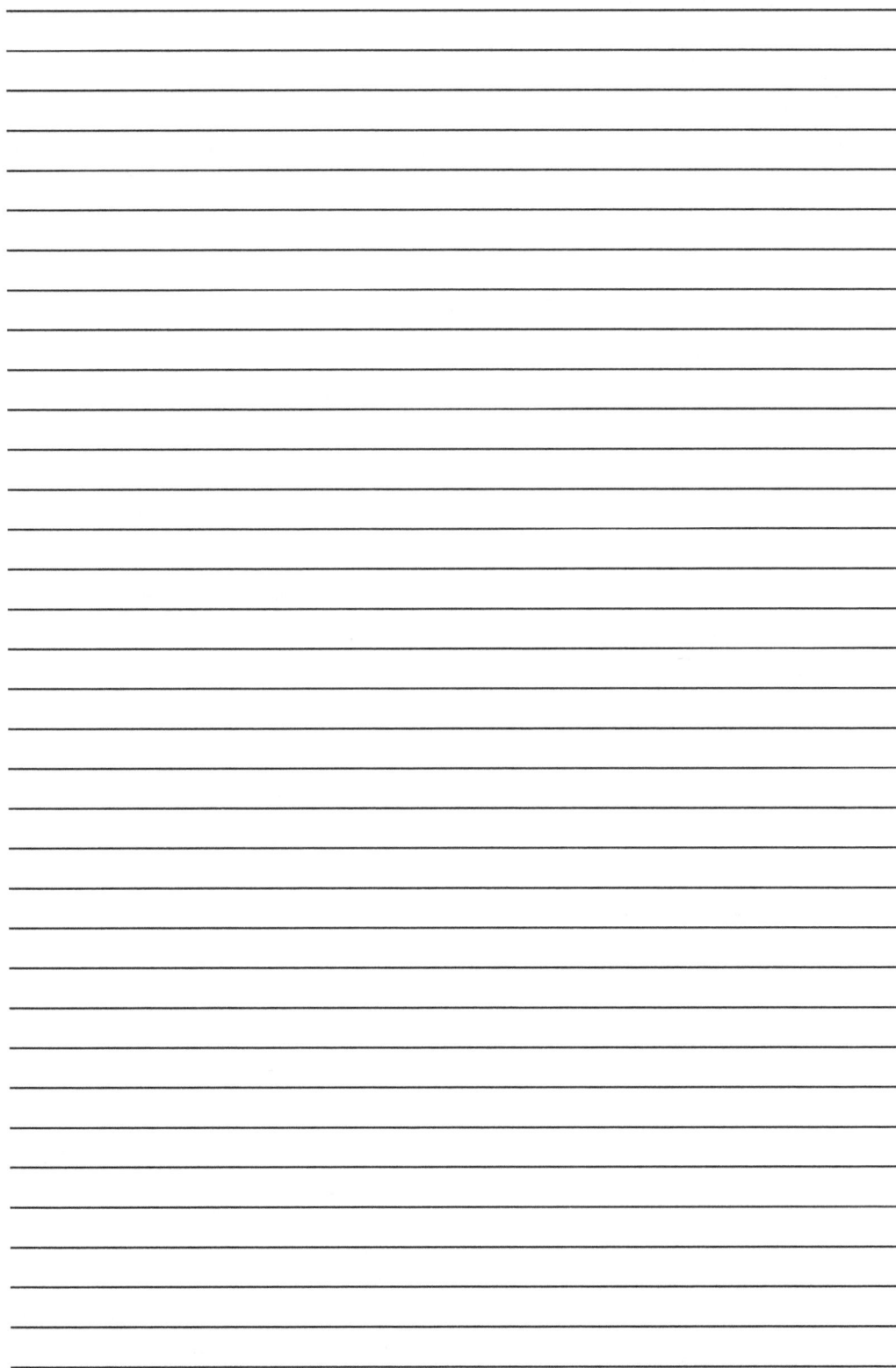

Hope for the Future

Whether or not you have your own children or grandchildren, what hopes do you have for today's children? We all have something invested in the future, whether it is the future of our society, country, religion, culture, or family. What do you hope the world is like in 50 years? In 100 years?

_____

_____

_____

_____

_____

_____

_____

_____

_____

_____

_____

_____

_____

_____

_____

_____

_____

_____

_____

_____

_____

_____

_____

_____

_____

_____

_____

_____

Hope and Joy

Attach an image, drawing, or keepsake that symbolizes your hope for the future. Does your hope lie in a child or young person in your life? What do you hope for this person? Does your hope lie in a group, an organization, a philosophy, or an ideal? How might people bring hope or joy and improve the world? What hope do you hold for the future? Explain the image below.

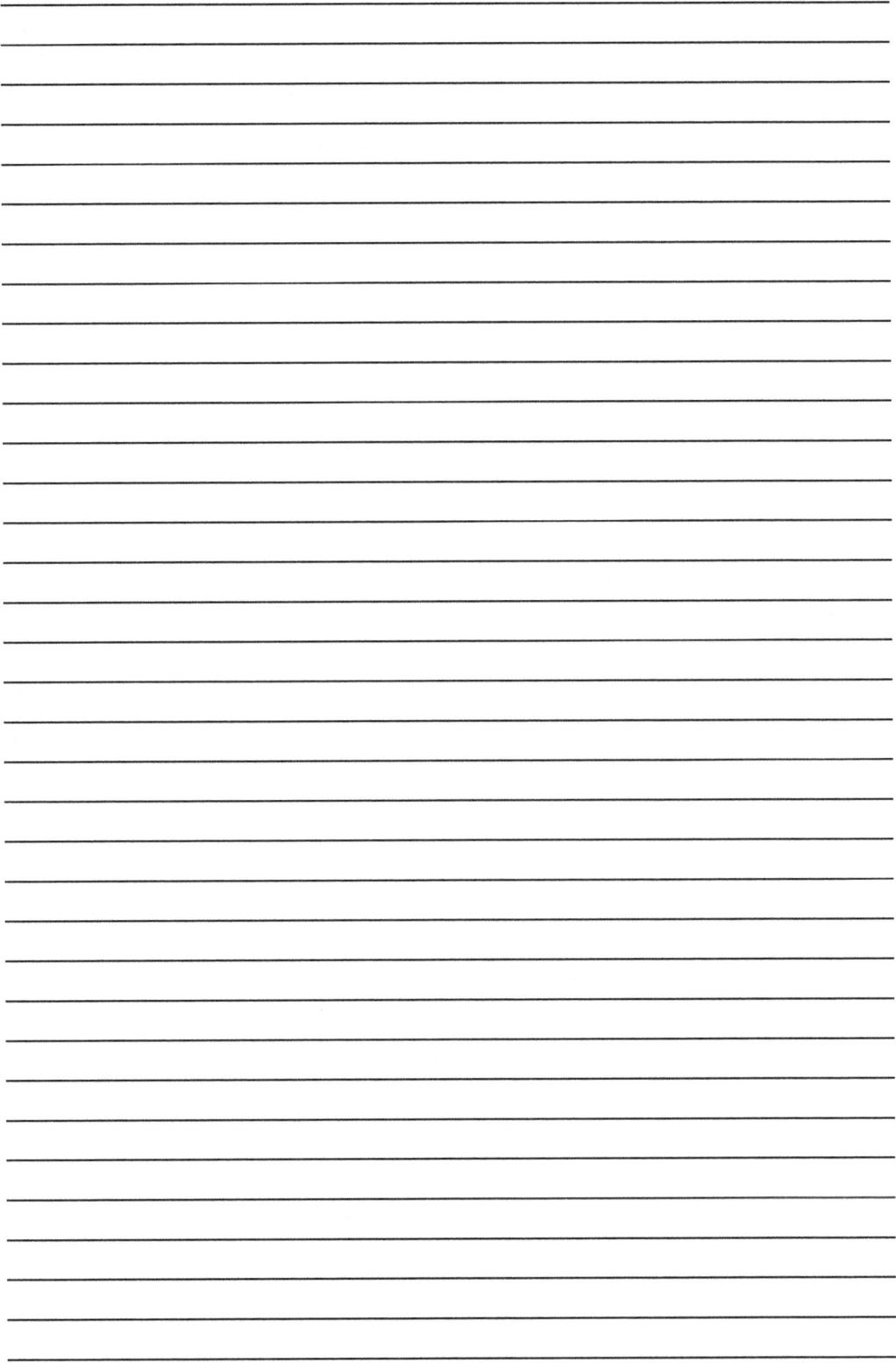

The Pitter Patter of Little Feet

Share a story about children, either your own children or your nieces and nephews or someone else's children. Do you recall a time when a child did something hilarious, thoughtful, or exceptional? How have children affected you throughout your life?

_____

_____

_____

_____

_____

_____

_____

_____

_____

_____

_____

_____

_____

_____

_____

_____

_____

_____

_____

_____

_____

_____

_____

_____

_____

_____

_____

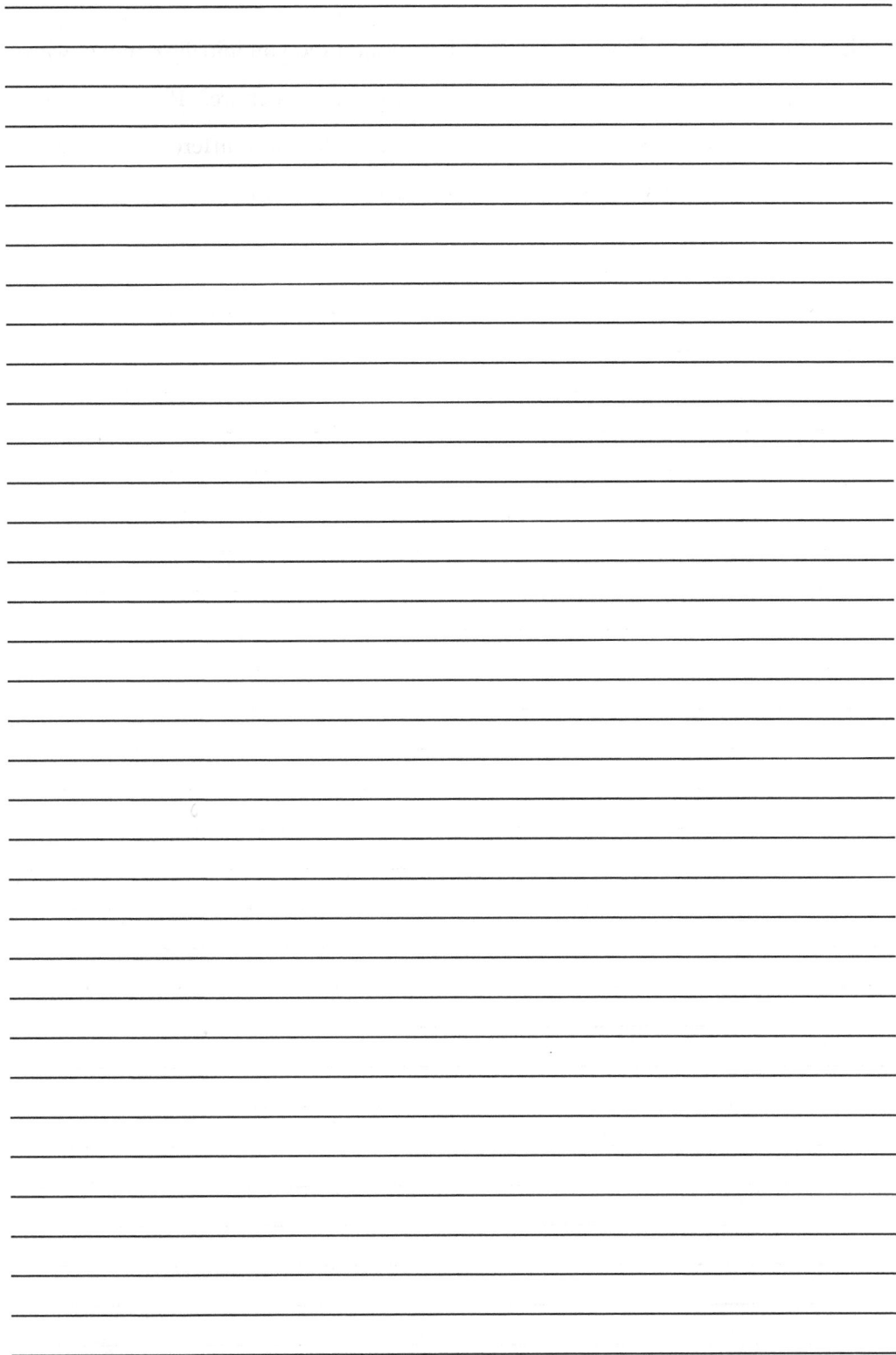

Meaningful Work

Explain the importance of your career. What about it did you initially connect with? What about your career do you love, and what aspects are a chore? If you could do it all over again, would you choose the same career or follow a different path? What about your career gives you a sense of pride and accomplishment?

_____
_____
_____
_____
_____
_____
_____
_____
_____
_____
_____
_____
_____
_____
_____
_____
_____
_____
_____
_____
_____
_____
_____
_____
_____
_____
_____

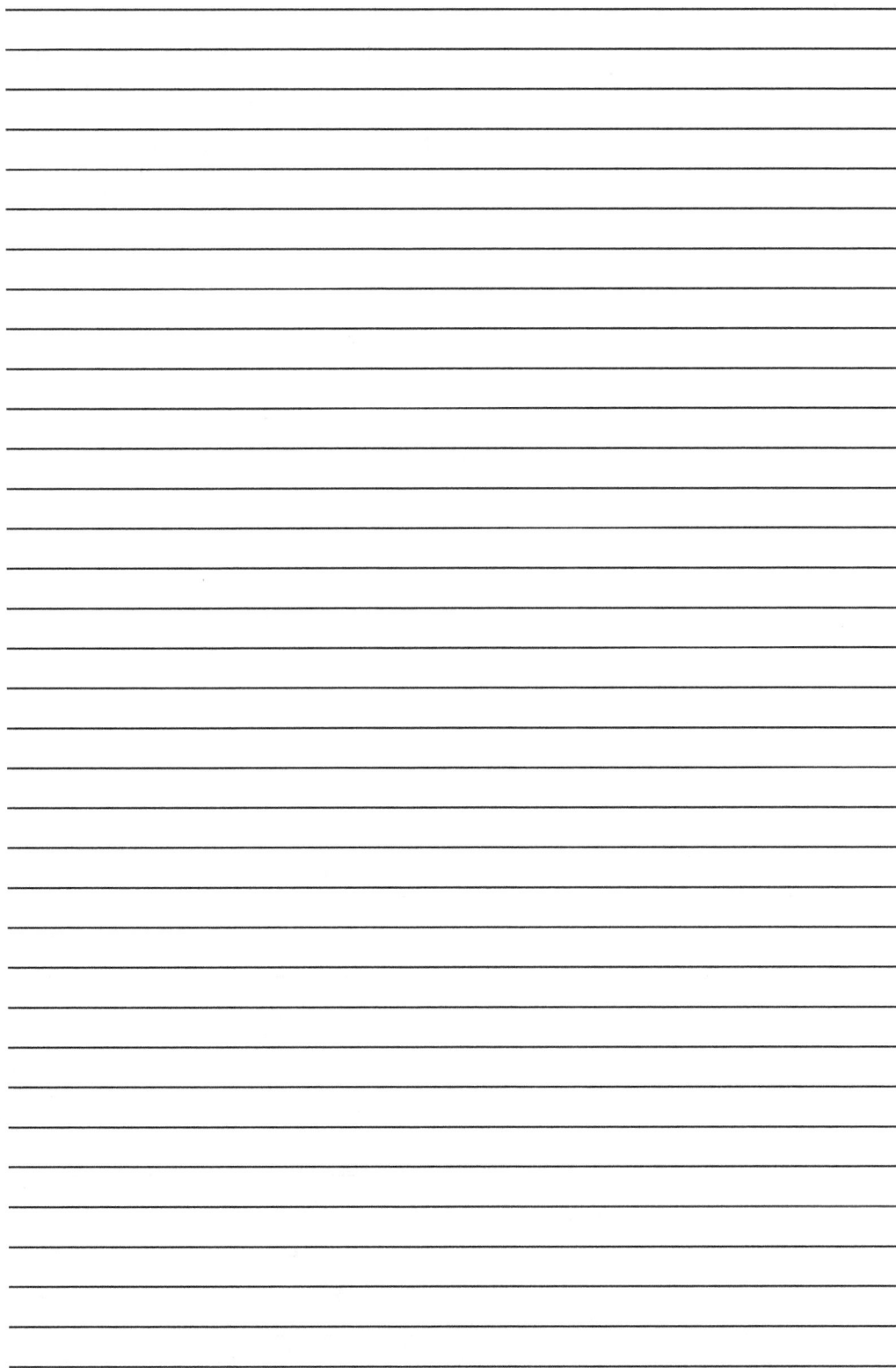

The Age of Technology

When did you begin to learn modern technical skills like working on a computer, a cell phone, and other devices? What were your thoughts of the first personal computers? Did you expect that people would each have a personal computer, then later on a laptop, cell phone, and other devices? Did you think that our society would become as dependent on technology as we are now? Where do you think technology will lead us in the next century? What is your relationship with technology and how do you choose to engage with it?

_____

_____

_____

_____

_____

_____

_____

_____

_____

_____

_____

_____

_____

_____

_____

_____

_____

_____

_____

_____

_____

_____

_____

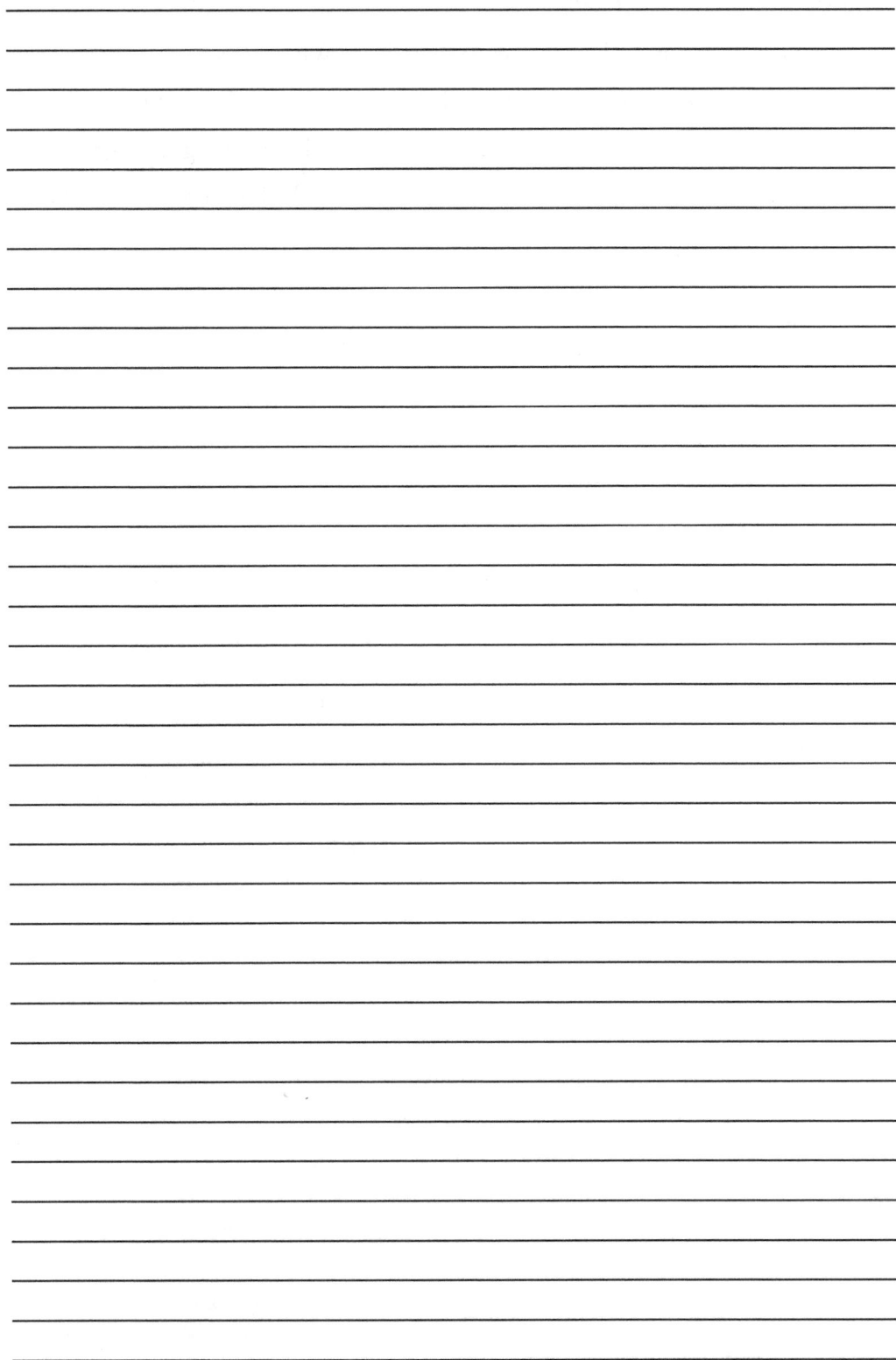

Overcoming our Challenges

All people face hardship and challenges in their lives. What steps have you taken to overcome adversity in your life? What has helped you conquer hard times and get you through difficult days? What advice can you share about getting through the challenges of life? What was the hardest choice you ever had to make? What made it so hard and how did you get through it?

_____

_____

_____

_____

_____

_____

_____

_____

_____

_____

_____

_____

_____

_____

_____

_____

_____

_____

_____

_____

_____

_____

_____

_____

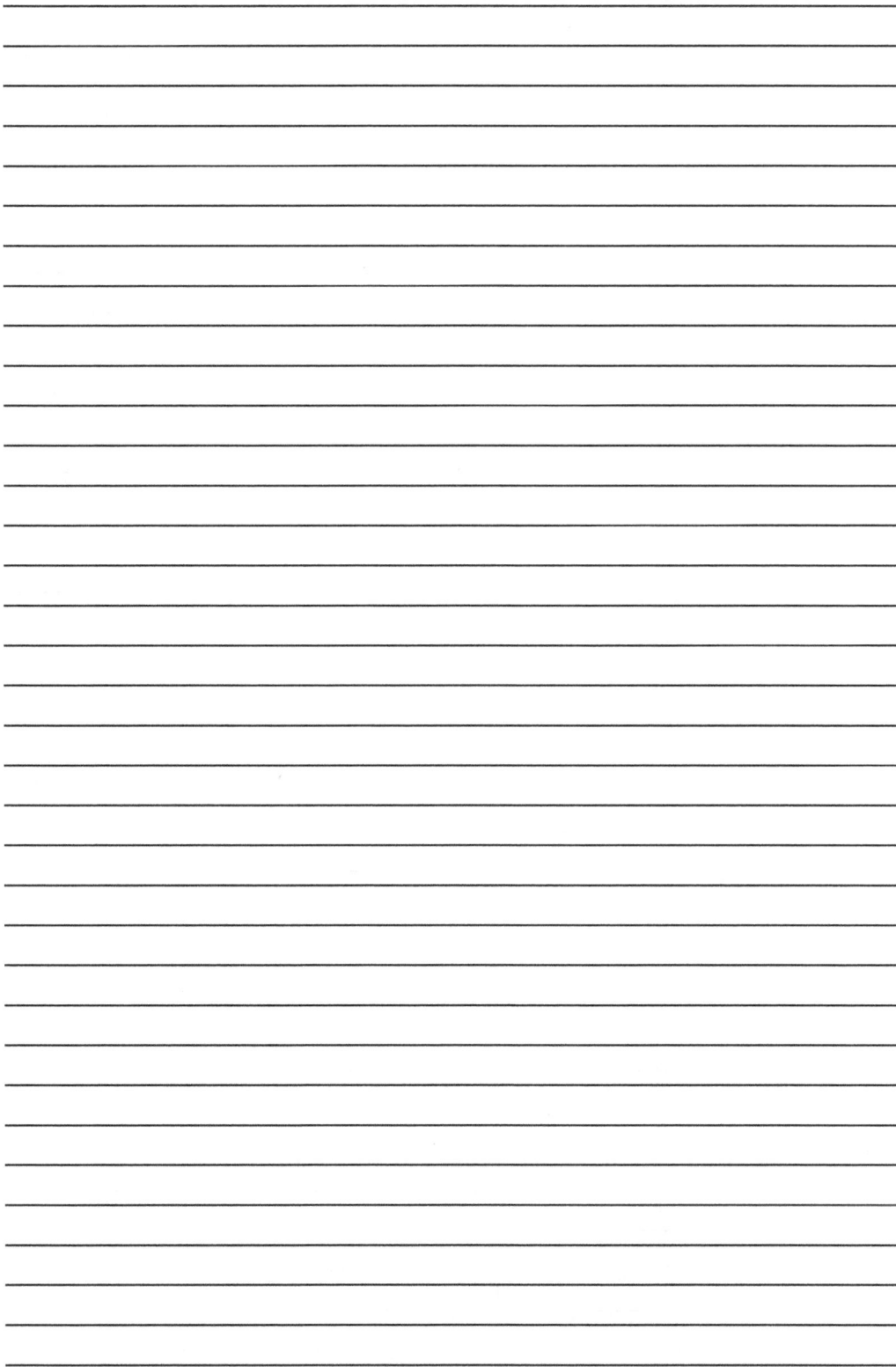

Holidays and Celebrations

What are your favorite holidays and why? What traditions do you celebrate? Do you have particular holiday ceremonies, meals, or decorations that are important to your celebrations? What is the perfect holiday like for you? Share a story of a memorable holiday.

_____

_____

_____

_____

_____

_____

_____

_____

_____

_____

_____

_____

_____

_____

_____

_____

_____

_____

_____

_____

_____

_____

_____

_____

_____

_____

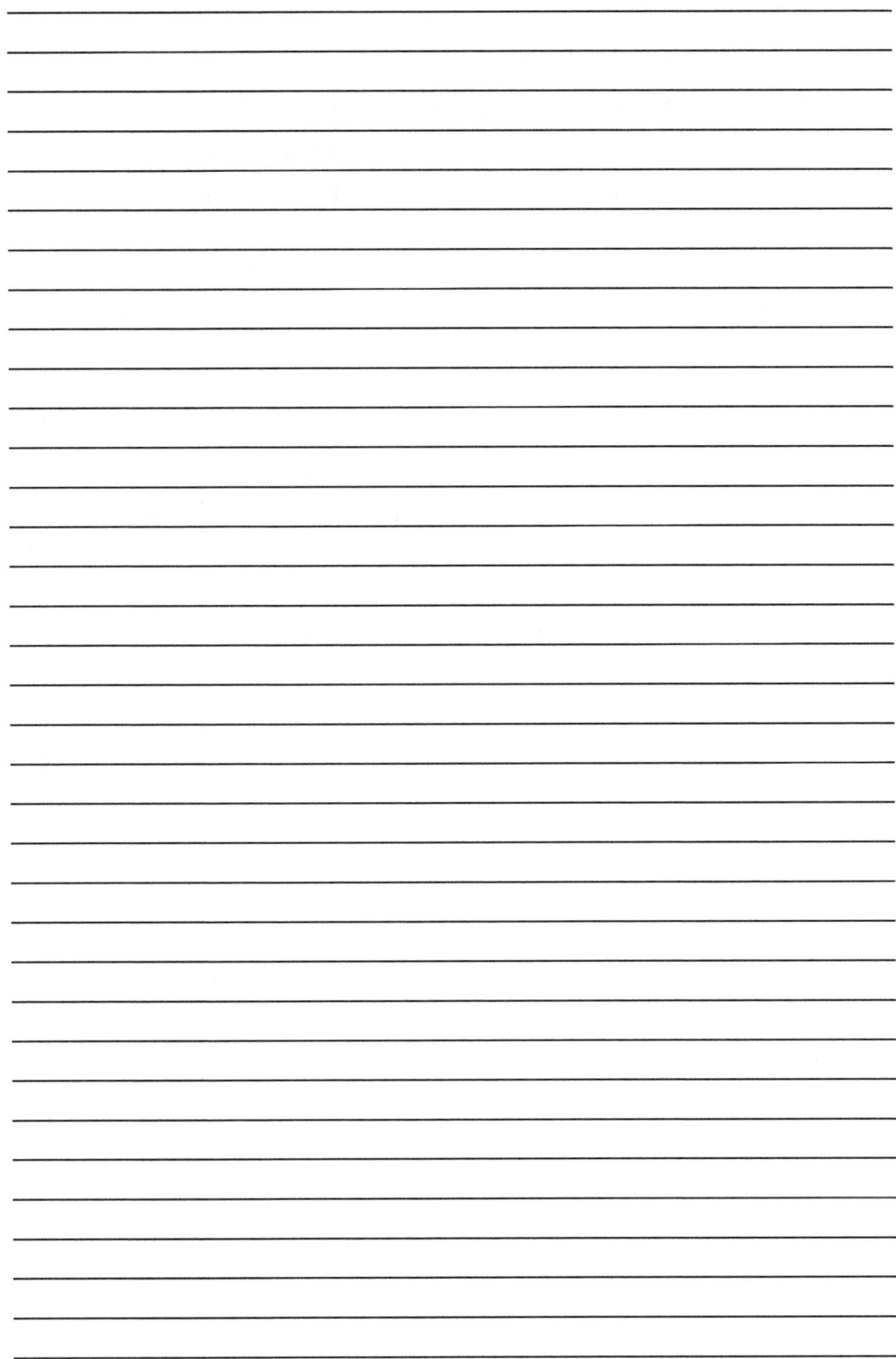

Keepsakes over Time

Attach a photograph, image, drawing, or keepsake of something that you cherish. This could be a Polaroid of your first car that made you fall in love with hot rods. It may be a snapshot of a loved one who stood by you through thick and thin. It may be a keepsake like a concert ticket from your favorite band. Whatever it is, include your picture and explain it.

A Few of your Favorite Things

As an adult, what are your favorite things? Favorite colors, clothes, hobbies, flowers, and books? Share details of your favorites. What could you not live a day without? What objects do you look forward to appreciating each day? Is it your collection of vintage tea pots, the motorcycle in the garage, or your photo albums with decades of memories that make you excited to face the day?

_____

_____

_____

_____

_____

_____

_____

_____

_____

_____

_____

_____

_____

_____

_____

_____

_____

_____

_____

_____

_____

_____

_____

_____

_____

_____

_____

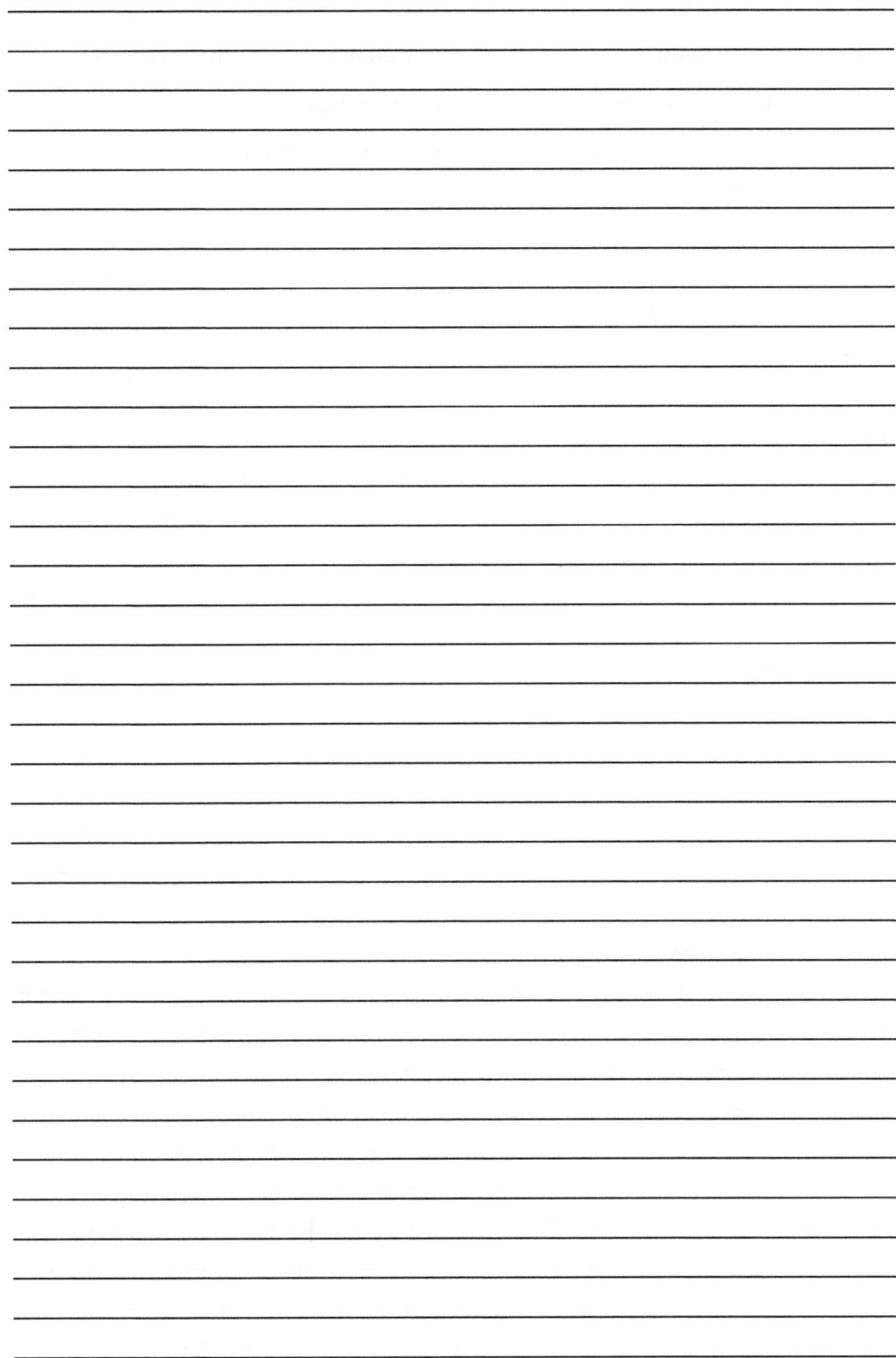

Just a Perfect Day

What would happen on a perfect day? Where would you go? What would you do?
Who would you spend a perfect day with? What would the weather be like? What
would you eat? What activities would you take part in? Include every little detail--
smells, tastes, sounds, and sights of the perfect day.

_____

_____

_____

_____

_____

_____

_____

_____

_____

_____

_____

_____

_____

_____

_____

_____

_____

_____

_____

_____

_____

_____

_____

_____

_____

_____

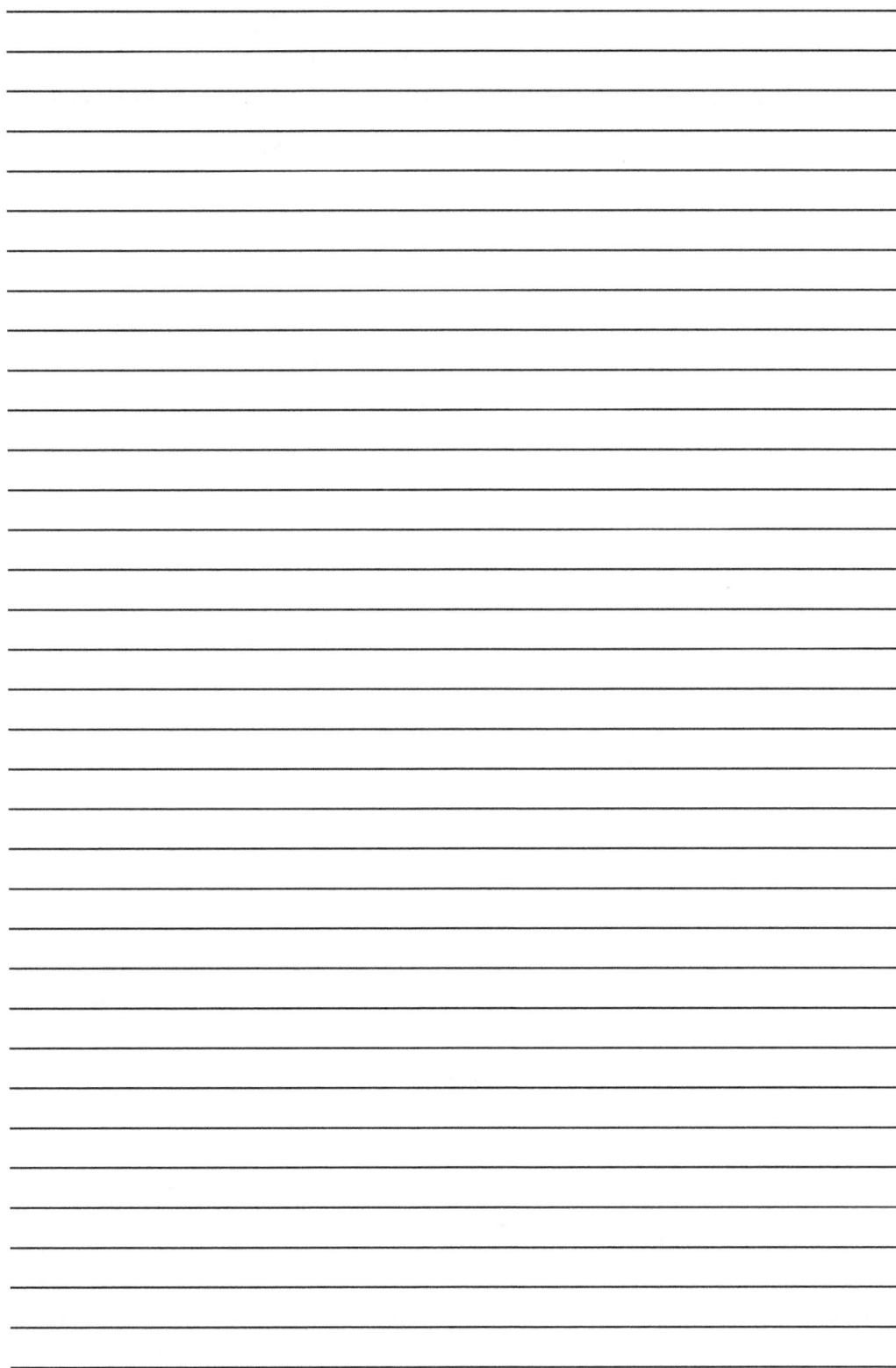

Around the World

Do you like to travel? Where have you been? What trips meant the most to you? What did you learn from traveling, and where would you still like to go? If you did not travel, what hobby or pastime has been meaningful to you? Describe it, and share what you love about it. How do you feel when you are involved in your hobby? What do you gain from it?

_____

_____

_____

_____

_____

_____

_____

_____

_____

_____

_____

_____

_____

_____

_____

_____

_____

_____

_____

_____

_____

_____

_____

_____

_____

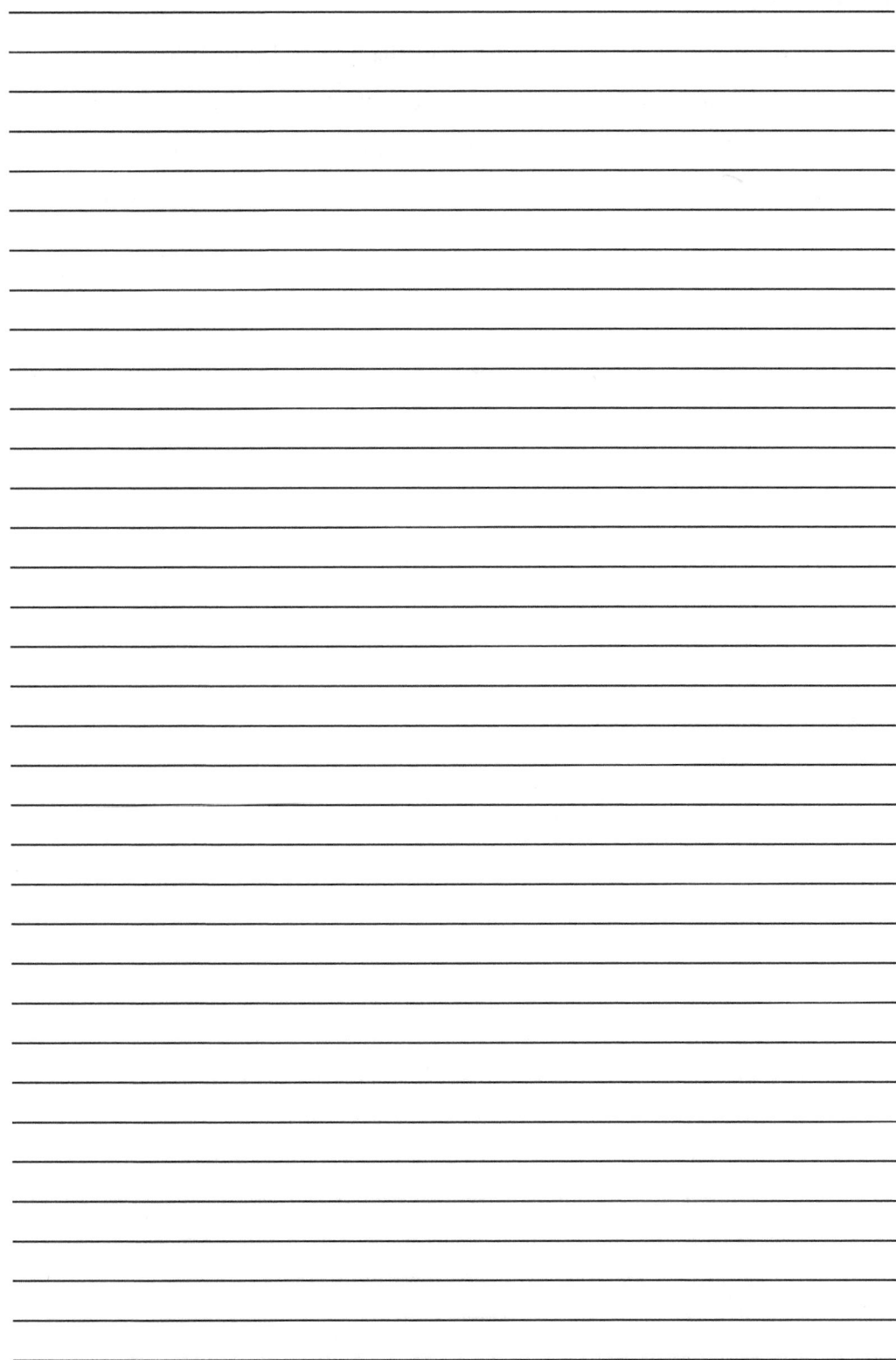

A Touching Event

Share a story of an event from your adult years that touched you. What happened in this event and what about it improved your life or the life of someone else? Who were you with? Did it change you in some way? Did it cause you to be more caring or understanding of another person? How did it help you grow or elevate your own humanity?

_____
_____
_____
_____
_____
_____
_____
_____
_____
_____
_____
_____
_____
_____
_____
_____
_____
_____
_____
_____
_____
_____
_____
_____

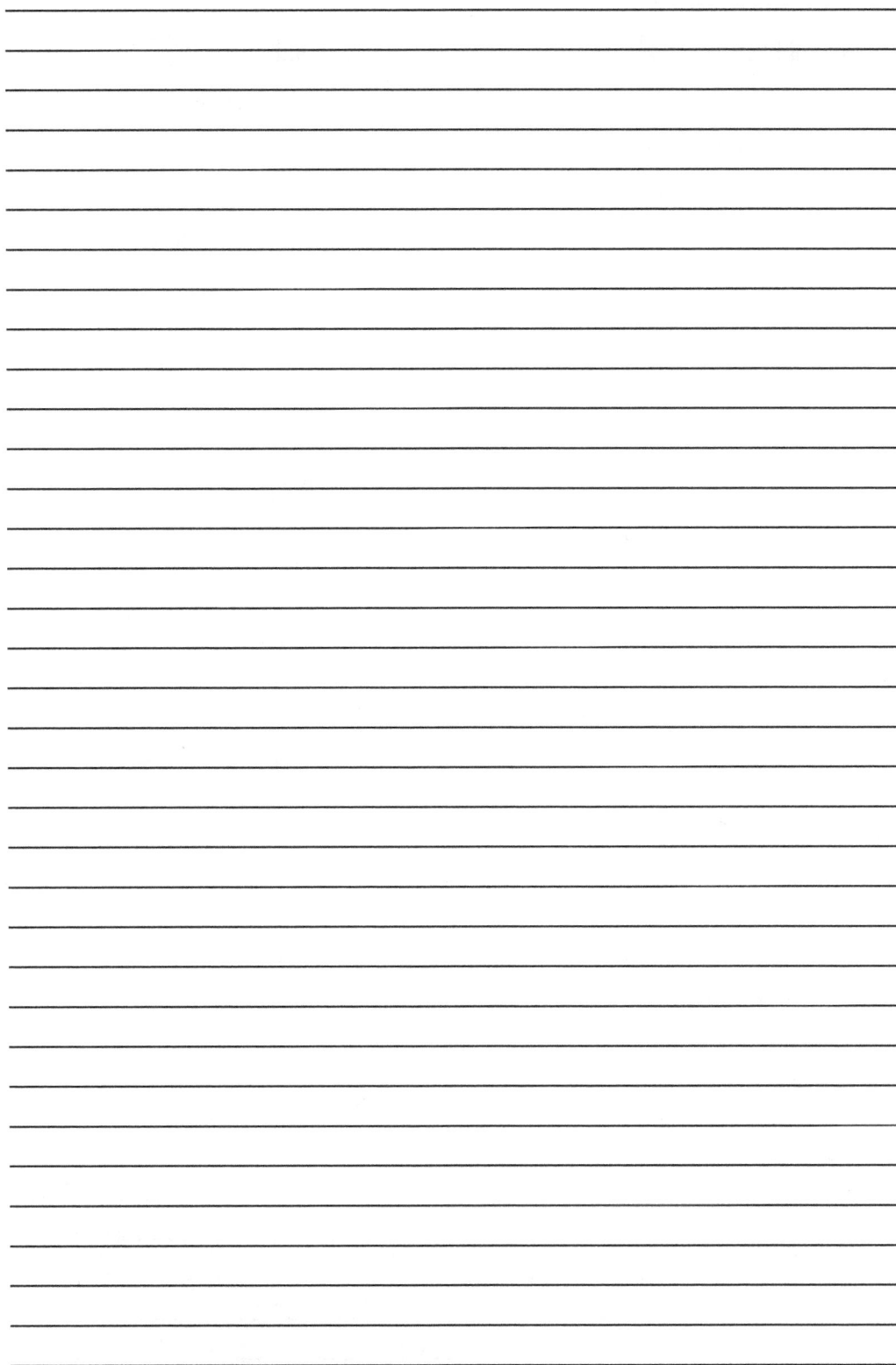

A Moment in History

If you could live in any time or place in history, what would it be? What historical time period is the most interesting? What about it do you value? What historical figures do you admire, and what do you like about them? Have people from history influenced your life? Have historical books (*The Autobiography of Benjamin Franklin* or *Walden* by Thoreau or *Silent Spring* by Rachel Carson) affected you? In what ways?

_____

_____

_____

_____

_____

_____

_____

_____

_____

_____

_____

_____

_____

_____

_____

_____

_____

_____

_____

_____

_____

_____

_____

_____

_____

_____

A Taste of the Good Life

Include your favorite recipe here. Maybe it is a cocktail that you make every year at the holidays. Perhaps it is your fudge recipe that you have kept secret all this time. It could be your famous cake recipe that makes everyone ask for more. Include your favorite recipe and a description of when you made this wonderful delicacy.

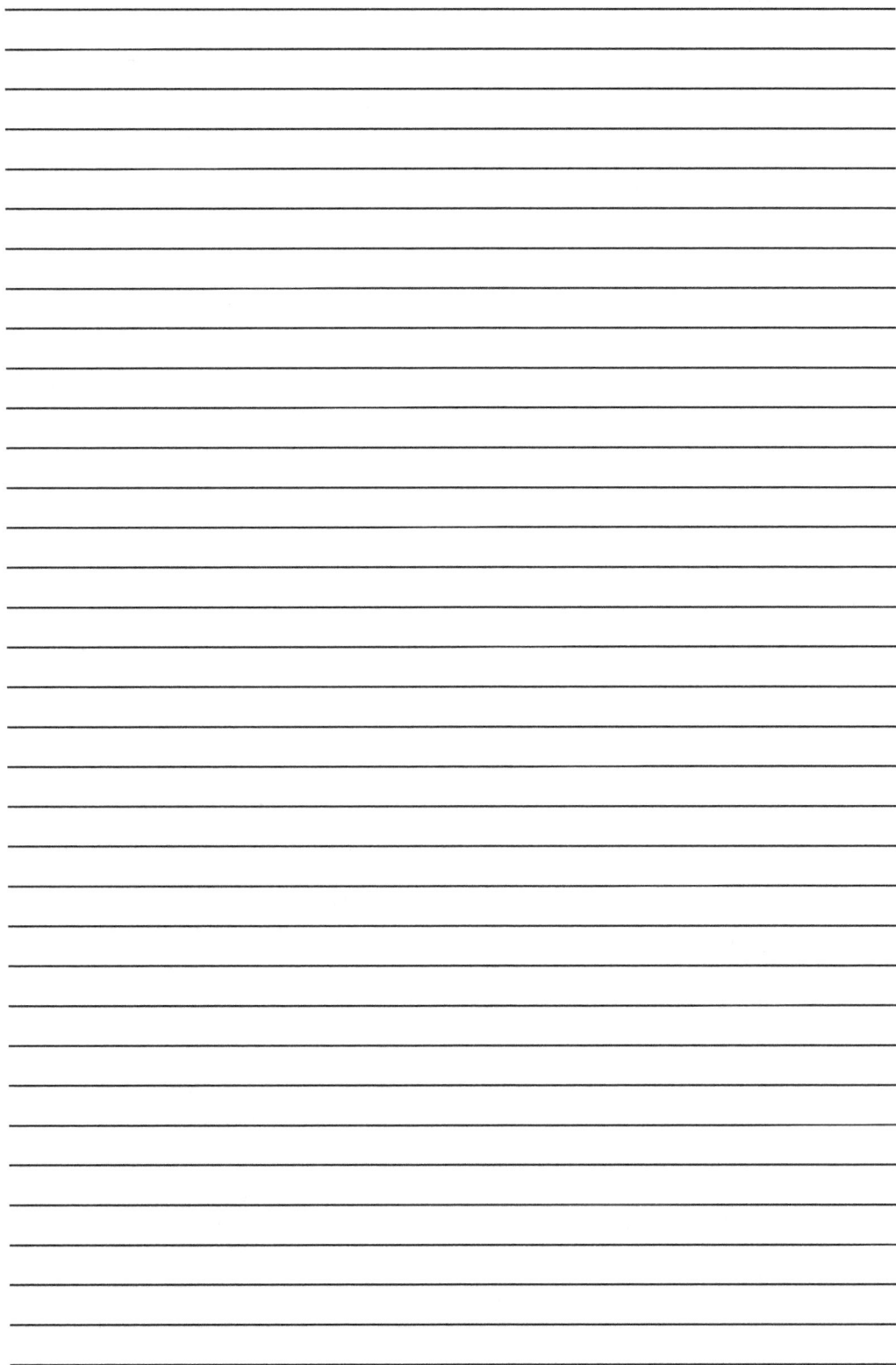

New Technologies

What have been the most useful inventions, innovations, or changes in your lifetime? What inventions changed life too much? What technological, political, or social changes do you think have created problems, and which ones have solved problems? What one thing in your life do you wish was there when you were a kid? What one thing do you miss the most? In what way has the world changed for the better? What innovations would you like to see?

_____

_____

_____

_____

_____

_____

_____

_____

_____

_____

_____

_____

_____

_____

_____

_____

_____

_____

_____

_____

_____

_____

_____

_____

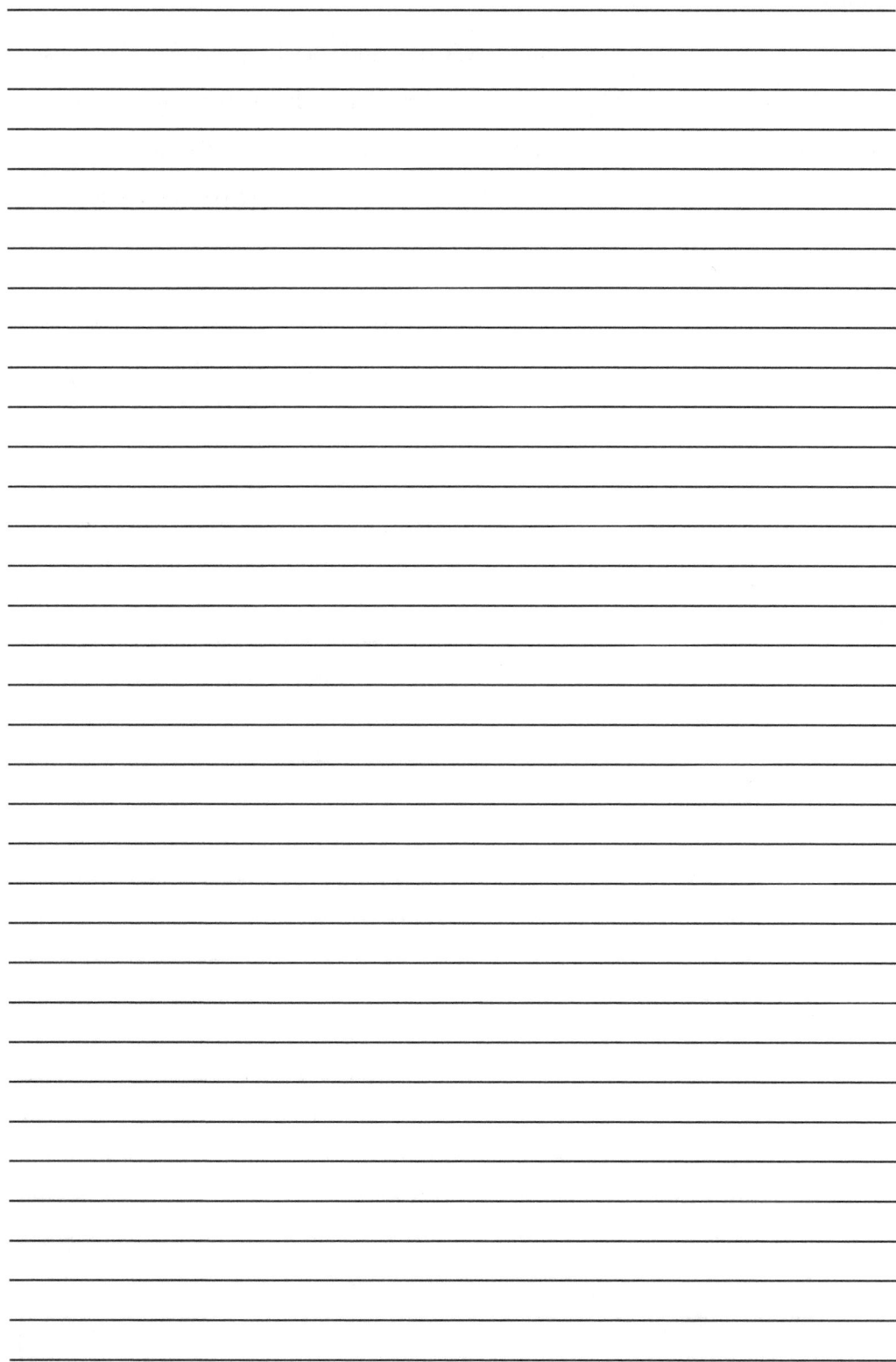

Personal Views

How would you describe your political, religious, and social viewpoints? Are those things important to you? Why or why not? Are there political, religious, or social leaders you admire? Are there leaders, living or dead, you would like to meet in person? What would you want to say or ask if you met a leader you admire in person?

_____

_____

_____

_____

_____

_____

_____

_____

_____

_____

_____

_____

_____

_____

_____

_____

_____

_____

_____

_____

_____

_____

_____

_____

_____

_____

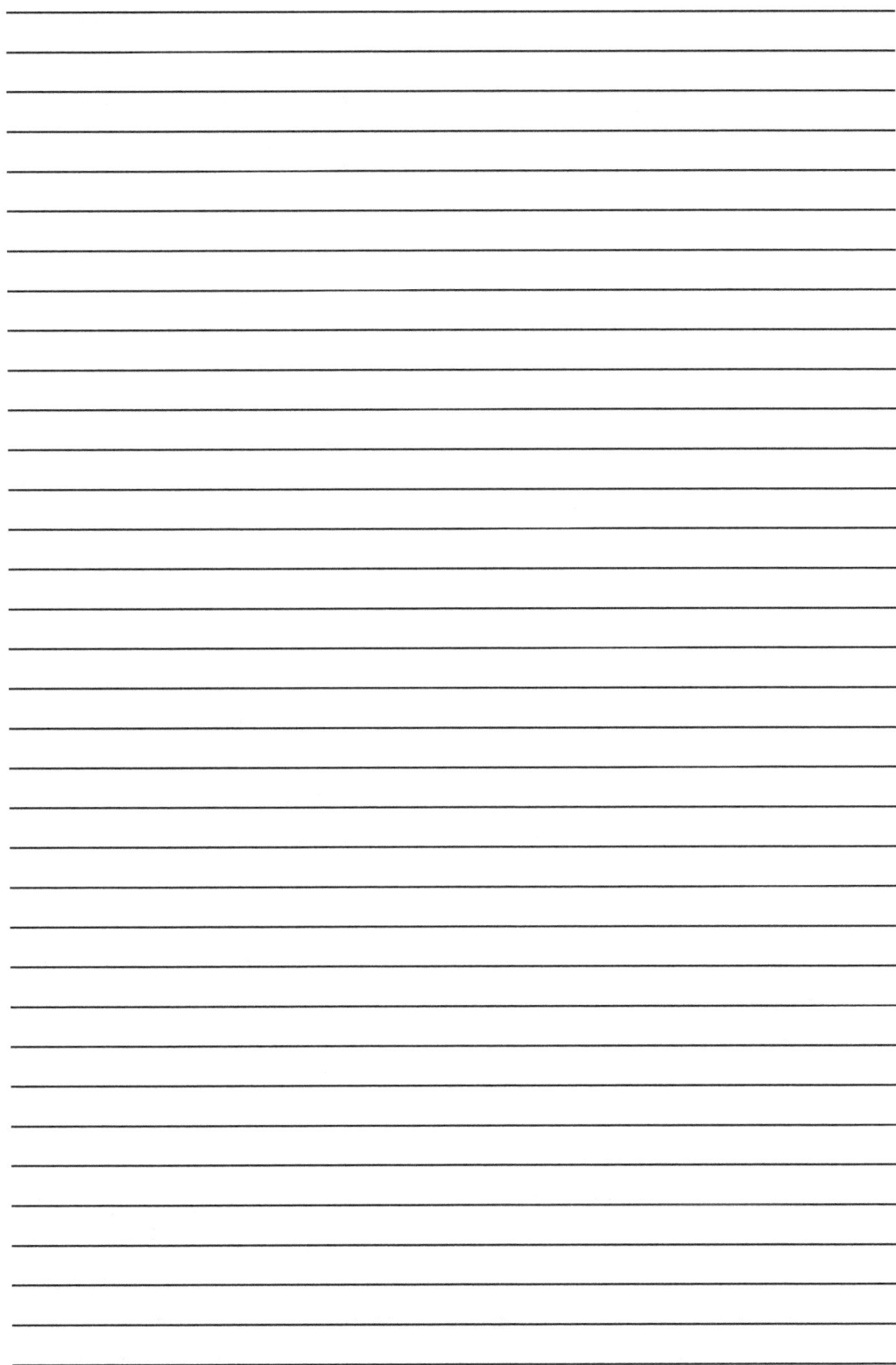

Creativity

What music, art, film, literature, or other types of creations do you enjoy? Do you consider yourself creative? What have you built or invented? Describe the creative activity that you enjoy most and explain how it enriches your life. What creative pursuit do you see other people involved in that you appreciate and admire? What do you like about it?

_____
_____
_____
_____
_____
_____
_____
_____
_____
_____
_____
_____
_____
_____
_____
_____
_____
_____
_____
_____
_____
_____
_____
_____
_____
_____
_____

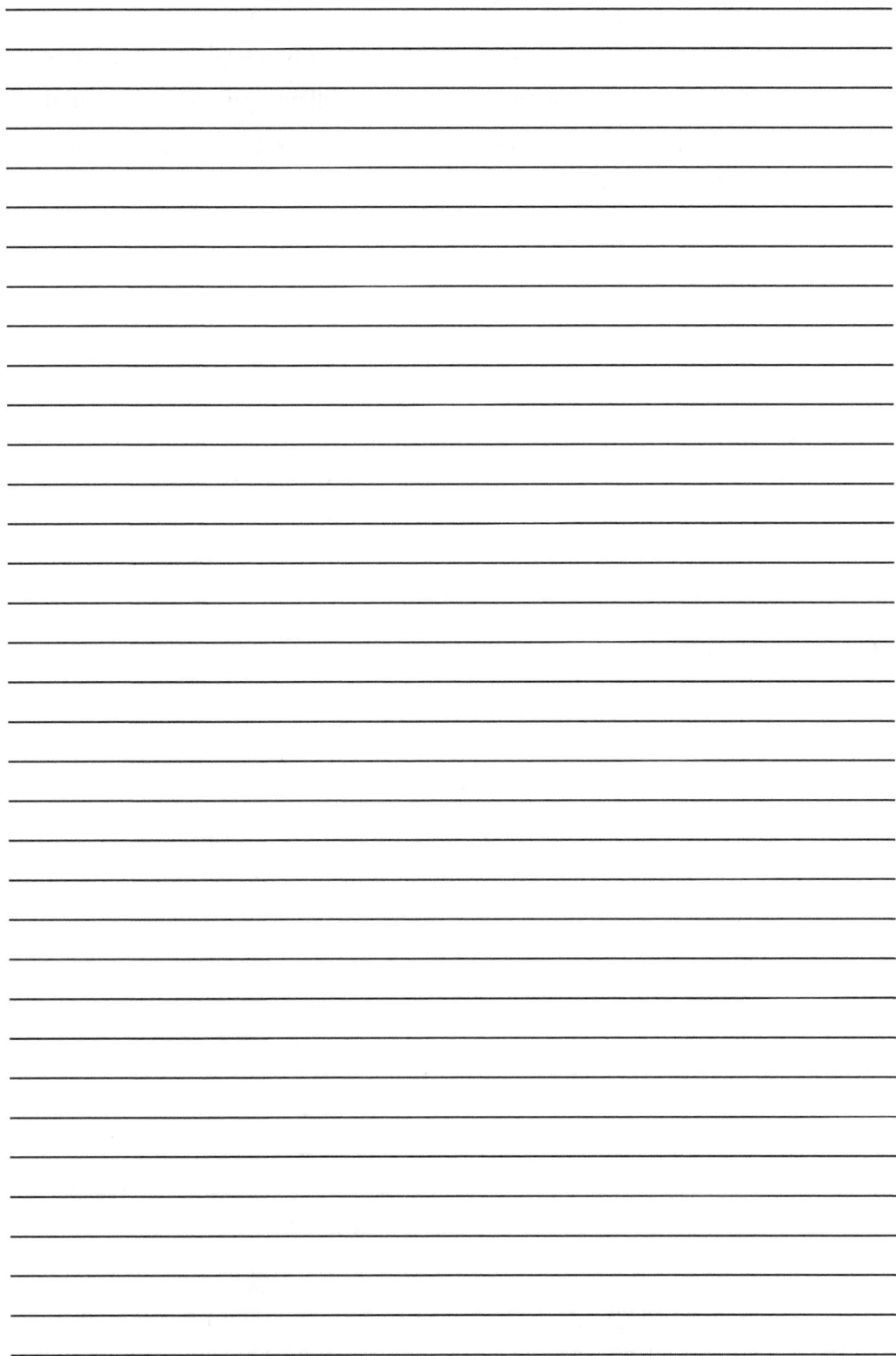

It's Just a Joke

Describe your sense of humor and sense of style. Do other people get your sense of humor most of the time or do your jokes sometimes fall on deaf ears? What kind of comedy or humor do you find to be most entertaining? Or do you think that people are too quick to crack a joke and need to be more serious? What is the best joke you've ever heard?

_____

_____

_____

_____

_____

_____

_____

_____

_____

_____

_____

_____

_____

_____

_____

_____

_____

_____

_____

_____

_____

_____

_____

What is Really Important?

What do you value most about your life? What could you not give up? What do you cherish and hold onto?   Is there anything on your bucket list that you would like to see, do, or accomplish? If you had a million dollars, perfect health, and no restrictions, what would you set off to do tomorrow?

_____

_____

_____

_____

_____

_____

_____

_____

_____

_____

_____

_____

_____

_____

_____

_____

_____

_____

_____

_____

_____

_____

_____

_____

_____

_____

_____

_____

_____

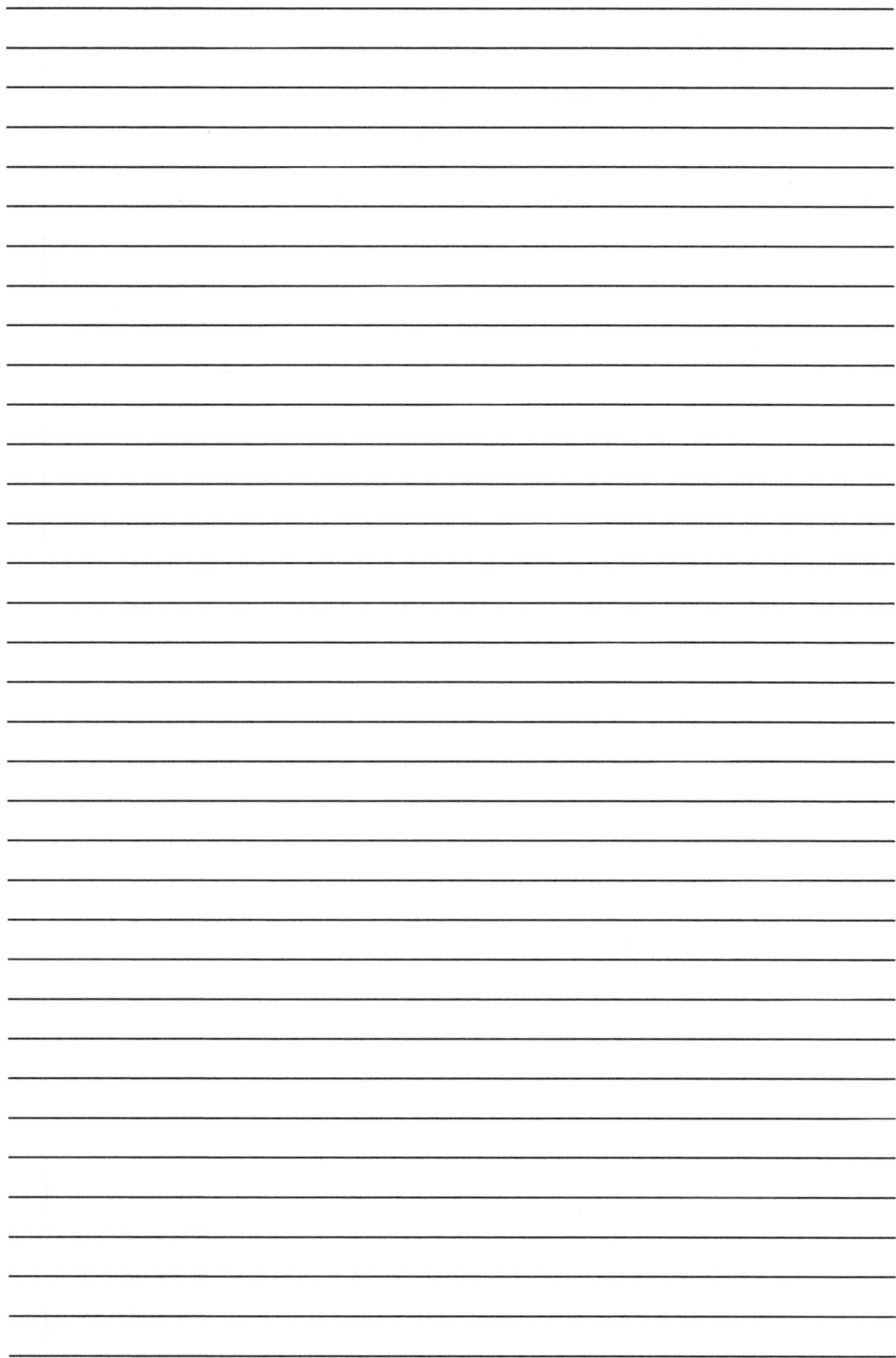

I Remember Poem

Write an I Remember Poem in the box below. Each line of the poem begins with the words "I Remember", and the rest is up to you.

I Believe Poem

Write an I Believe Poem in the box below. Each line of the poem begins with the words "I Believe", and the rest is up to you.

If You Had it to do All Over Again

If you could go back in time and do it all over again, what changes would you make? Would you go on that trip to Europe? Would you have asked the girl to dance? Would you have said "yes"? Would you have gotten the tattoo (or the wild outfit, the haircut, or the fast car)? Would you have taken a bigger risk? Would you have taken the road less traveled?

_____

_____

_____

_____

_____

_____

_____

_____

_____

_____

_____

_____

_____

_____

_____

_____

_____

_____

_____

_____

_____

_____

_____

_____

_____

_____

_____

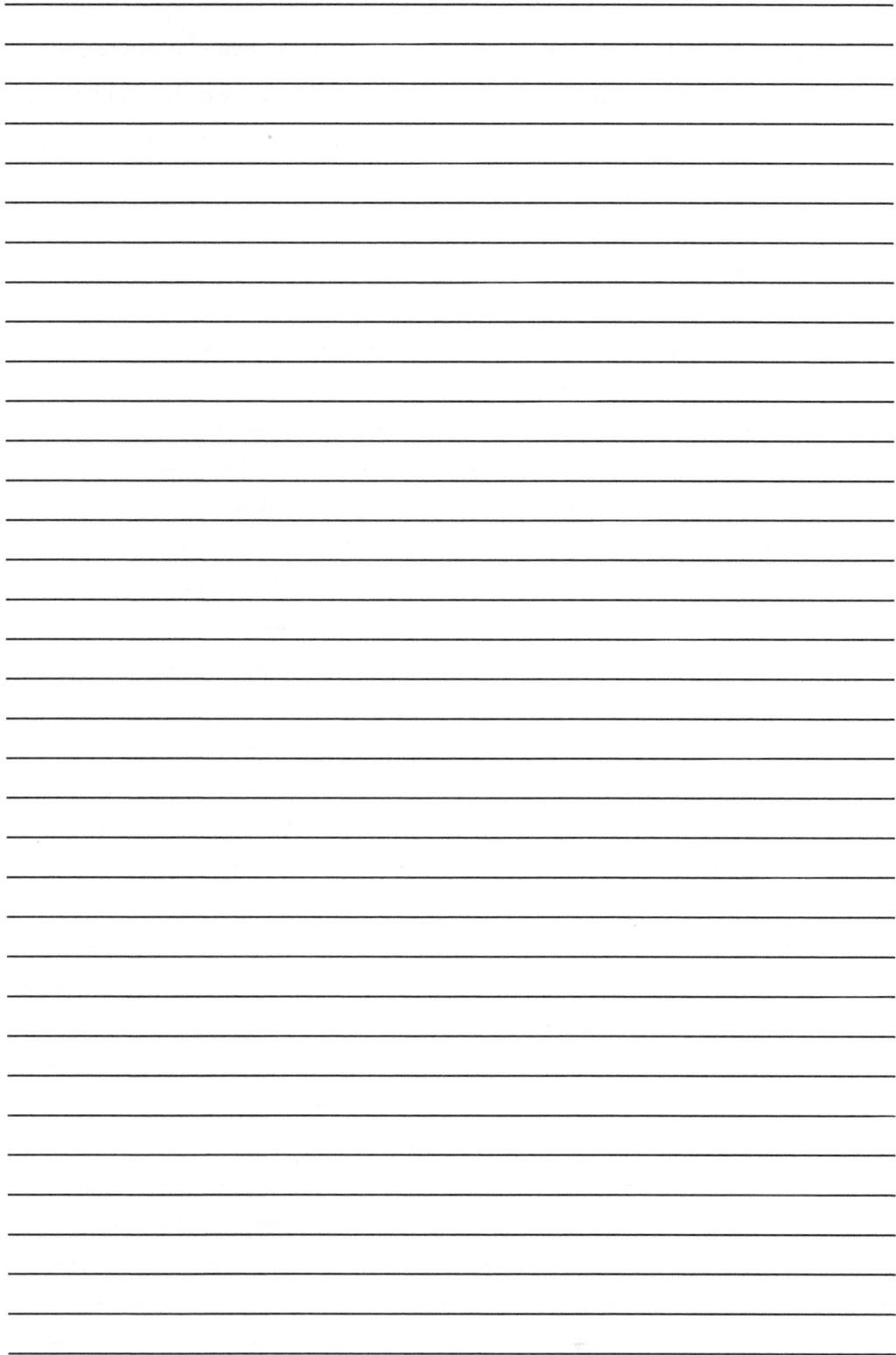

Your Legacy

What do you want to be remembered for? What accomplishments, attributes, or stories about you do you want people to remember? What five words would you like people to use to describe you? Why would you want them to think of you that way? What do you hope that people will pass on about you and share about you?

_____

_____

_____

_____

_____

_____

_____

_____

_____

_____

_____

_____

_____

_____

_____

_____

_____

_____

_____

_____

_____

_____

_____

_____

_____

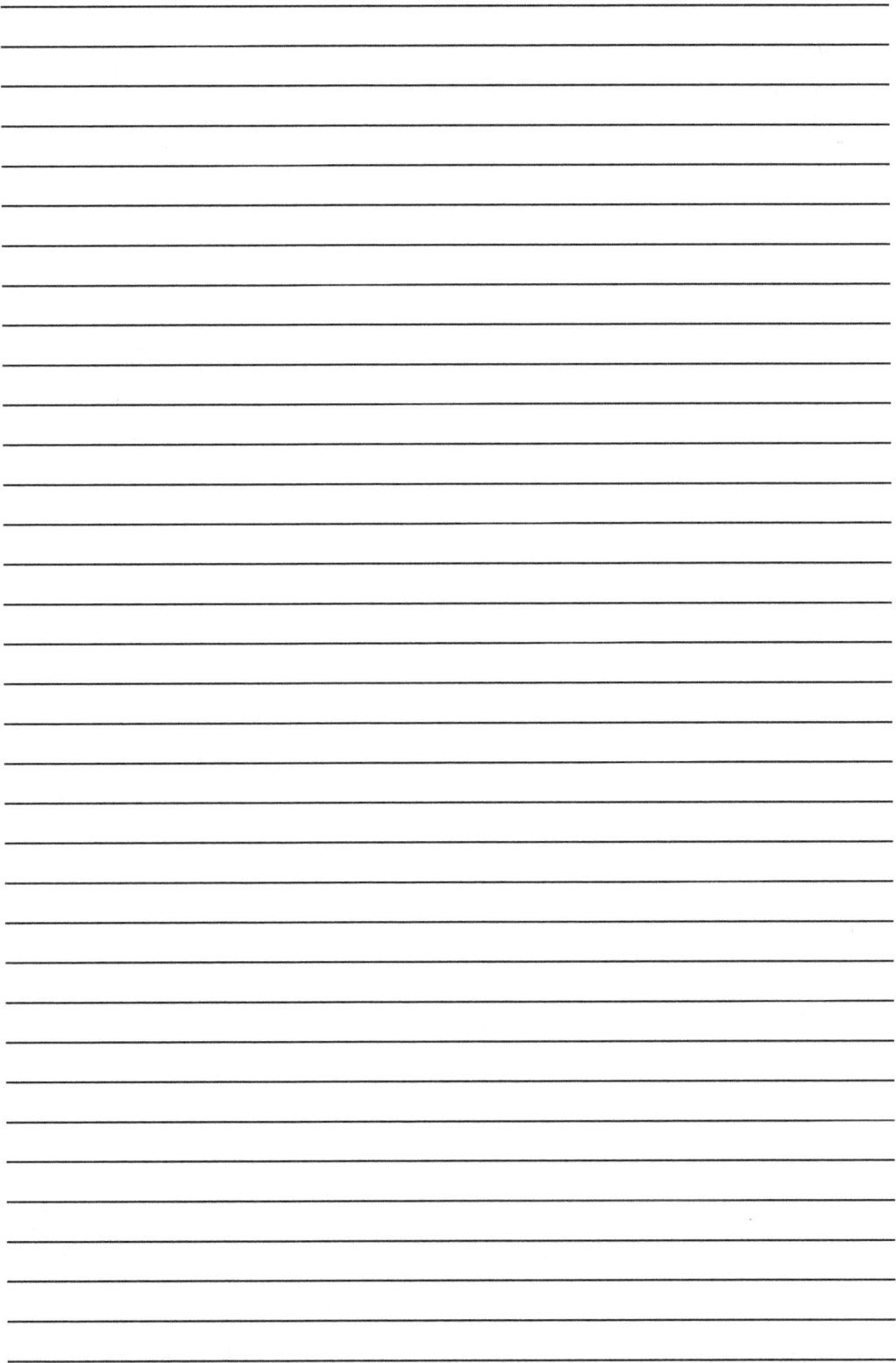

Cherished Message

What advice can you share about life? What would you like people to know? What do you wish people would understand and appreciate? If you could get one message out to your community, the country, or the world, what would it be? Why is this message so important to share? What events in your life led you to be passionate about this topic?

_____

_____

_____

_____

_____

_____

_____

_____

_____

_____

_____

_____

_____

_____

_____

_____

_____

_____

_____

_____

_____

_____

_____

_____

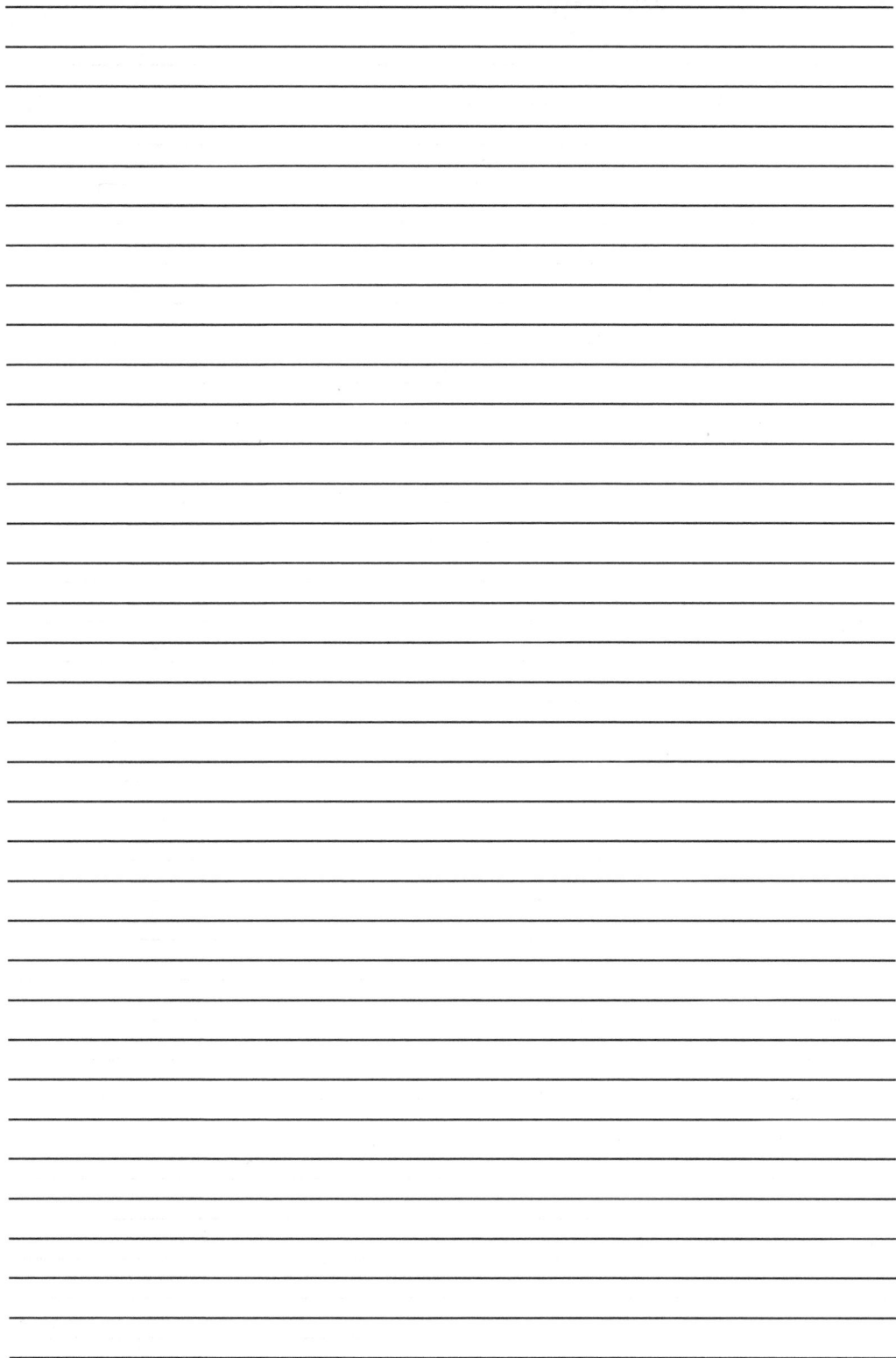

Share a story that you think should be remembered.

_____
_____
_____
_____
_____
_____
_____
_____
_____
_____
_____
_____
_____
_____
_____
_____
_____
_____
_____
_____
_____
_____
_____
_____
_____
_____
_____
_____
_____
_____

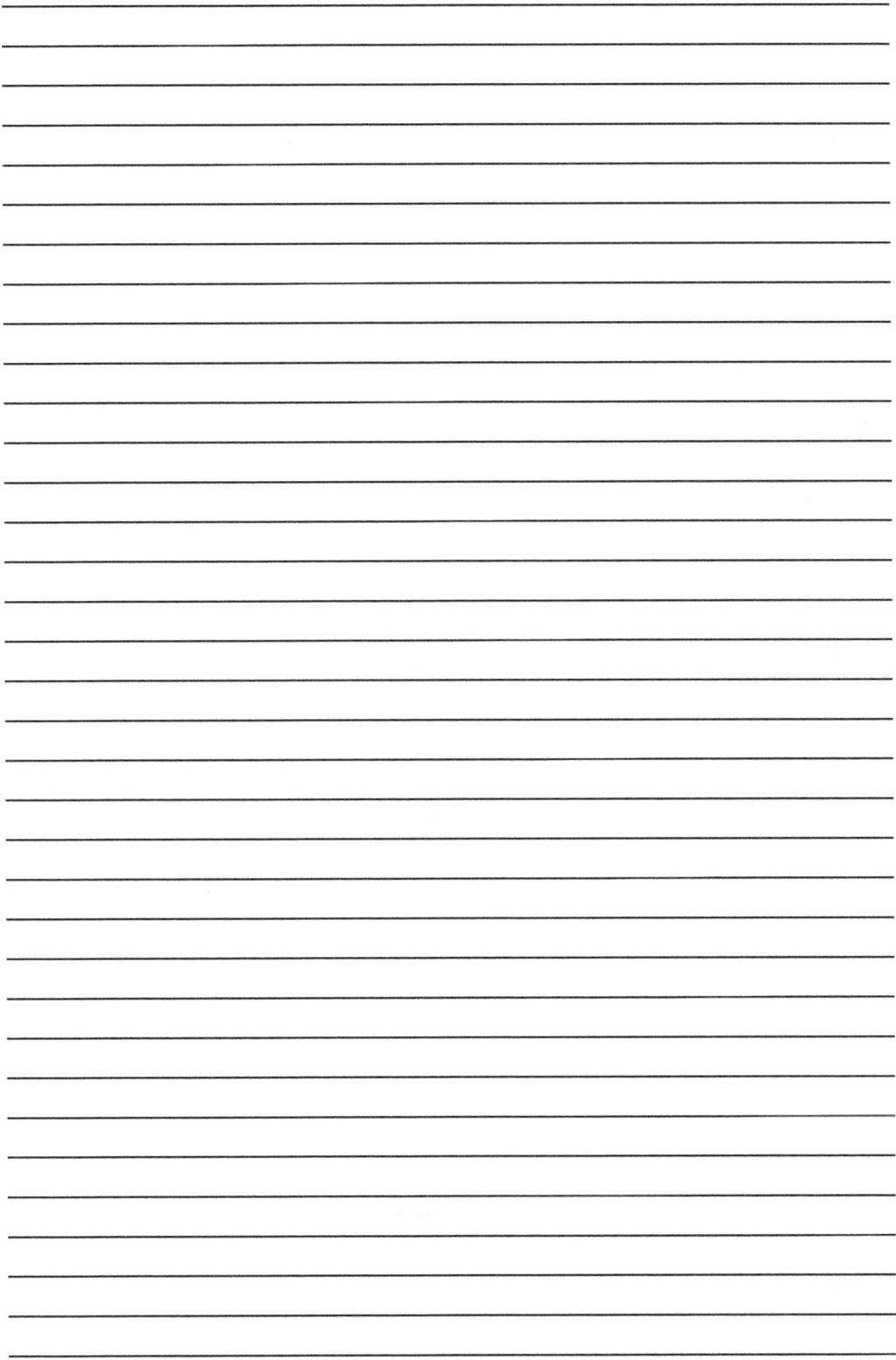

Share advice that could be helpful to other people.

_____
_____
_____
_____
_____
_____
_____
_____
_____
_____
_____
_____
_____
_____
_____
_____
_____
_____
_____
_____
_____
_____
_____
_____
_____
_____
_____
_____
_____
_____
_____

Share your opinions about a topic that is important to you.

_____

_____

_____

_____

_____

_____

_____

_____

_____

_____

_____

_____

_____

_____

_____

_____

_____

_____

_____

_____

_____

_____

_____

_____

_____

_____

_____

_____

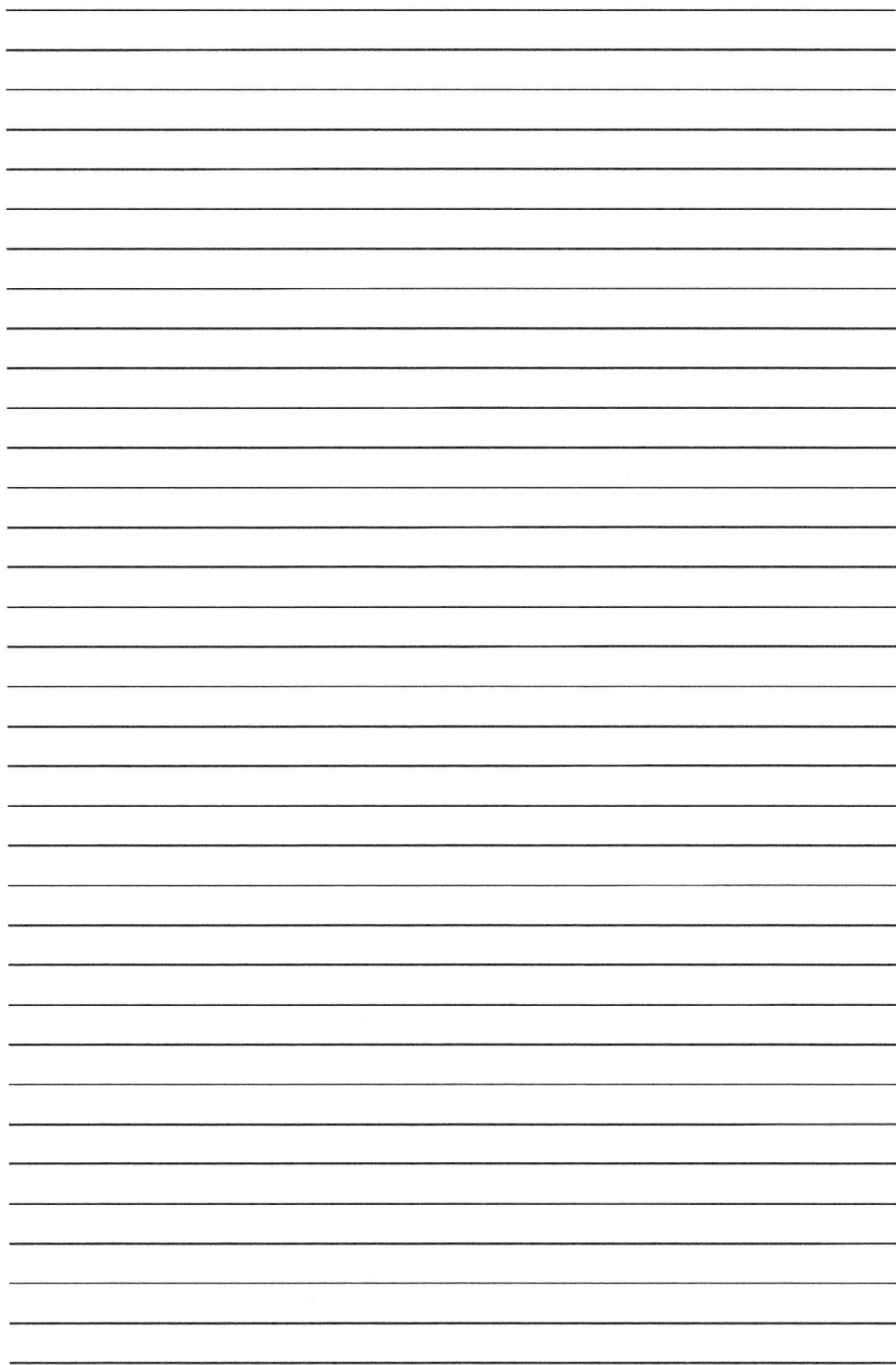

Share your favorite recipes, instructions, quotations, or teachings.

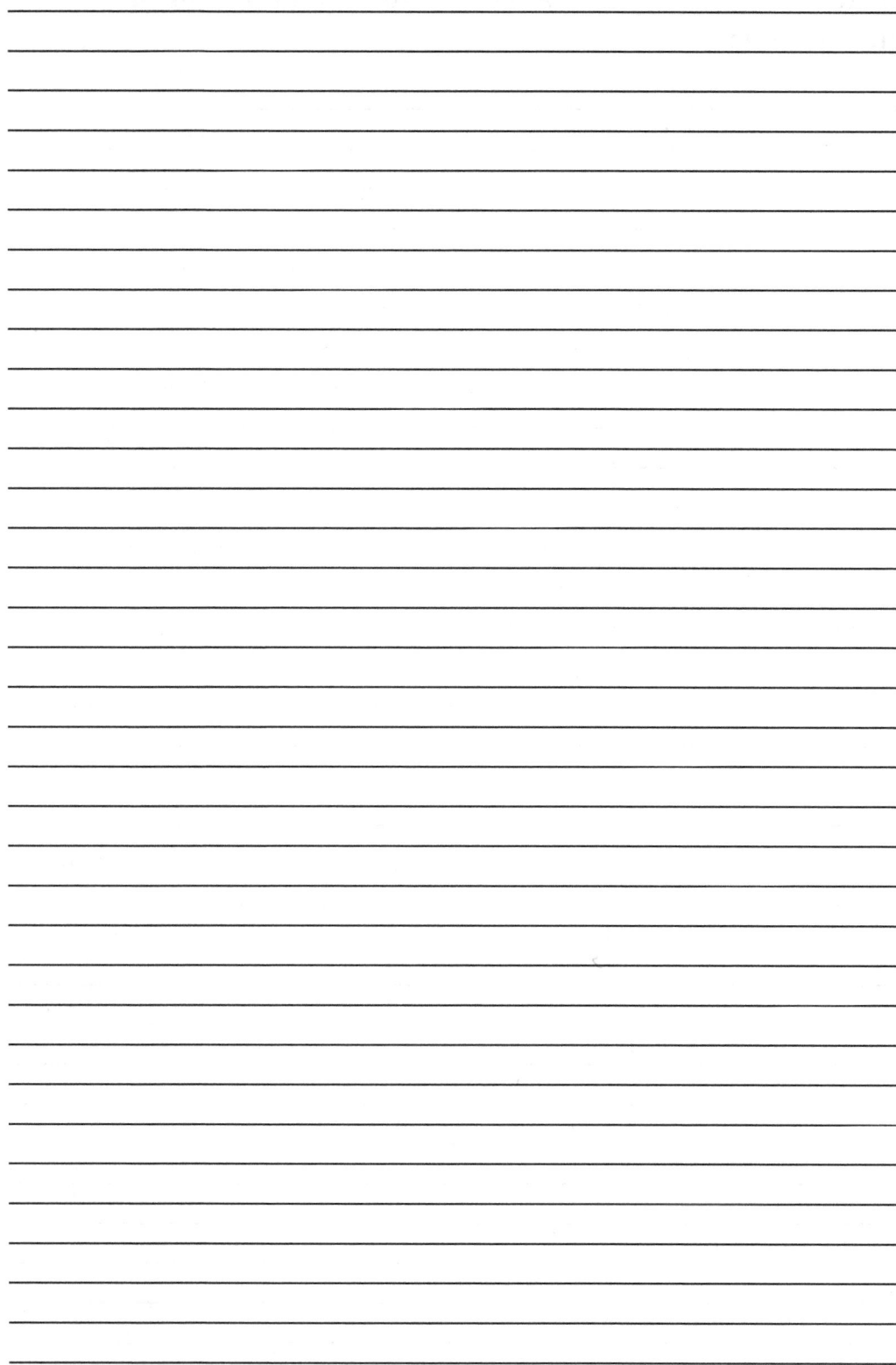

Share a favorite story that you heard about your parents or grandparents.

_____

_____

_____

_____

_____

_____

_____

_____

_____

_____

_____

_____

_____

_____

_____

_____

_____

_____

_____

_____

_____

_____

_____

_____

_____

_____

_____

_____

Share something that you should not have done but you did anyway.

_____
_____
_____
_____
_____
_____
_____
_____
_____
_____
_____
_____
_____
_____
_____
_____
_____
_____
_____
_____
_____
_____
_____
_____
_____
_____
_____
_____
_____
_____
_____
_____
_____

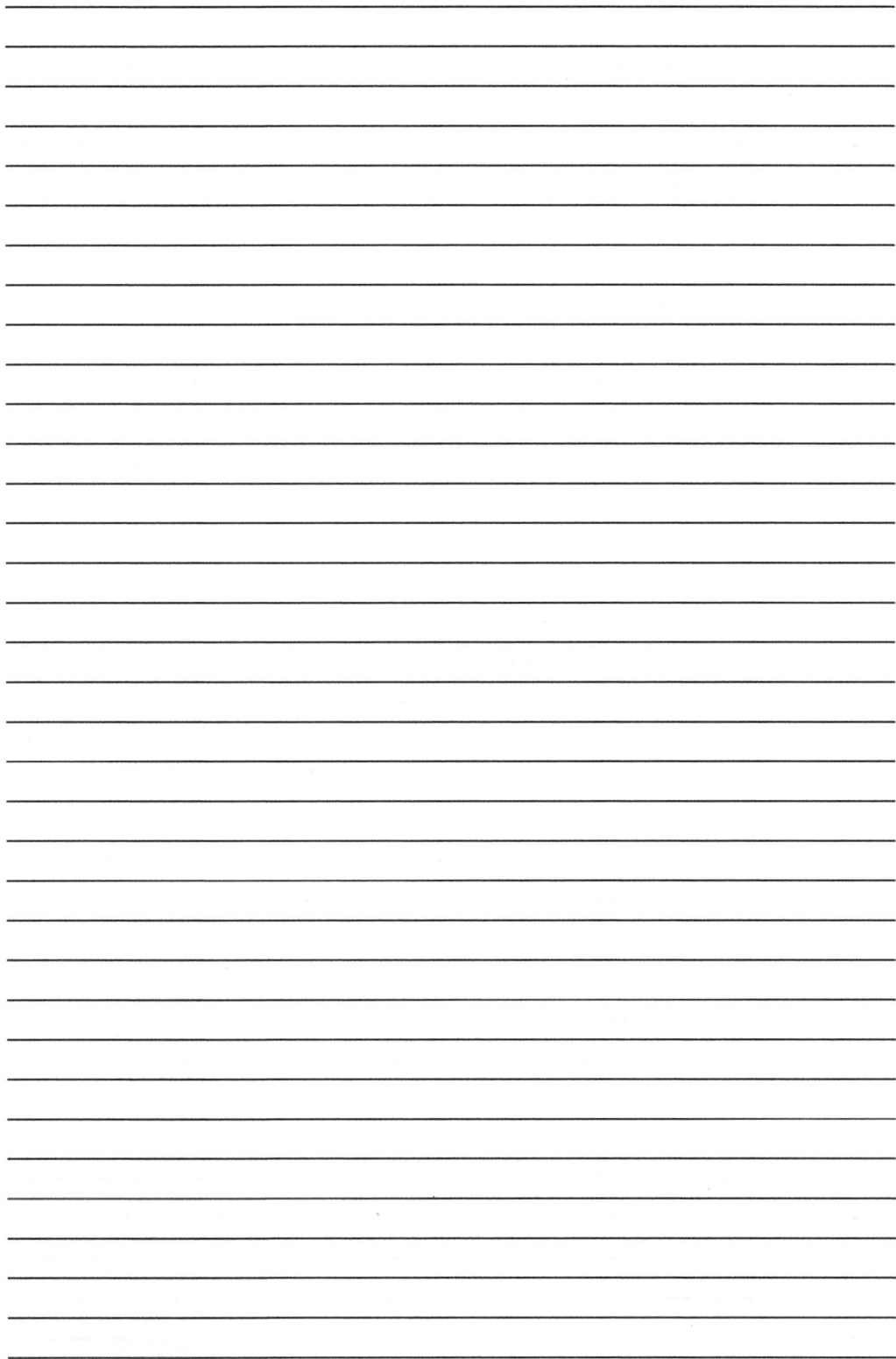

Share your favorite smells, sights, sounds, tastes, and textures.

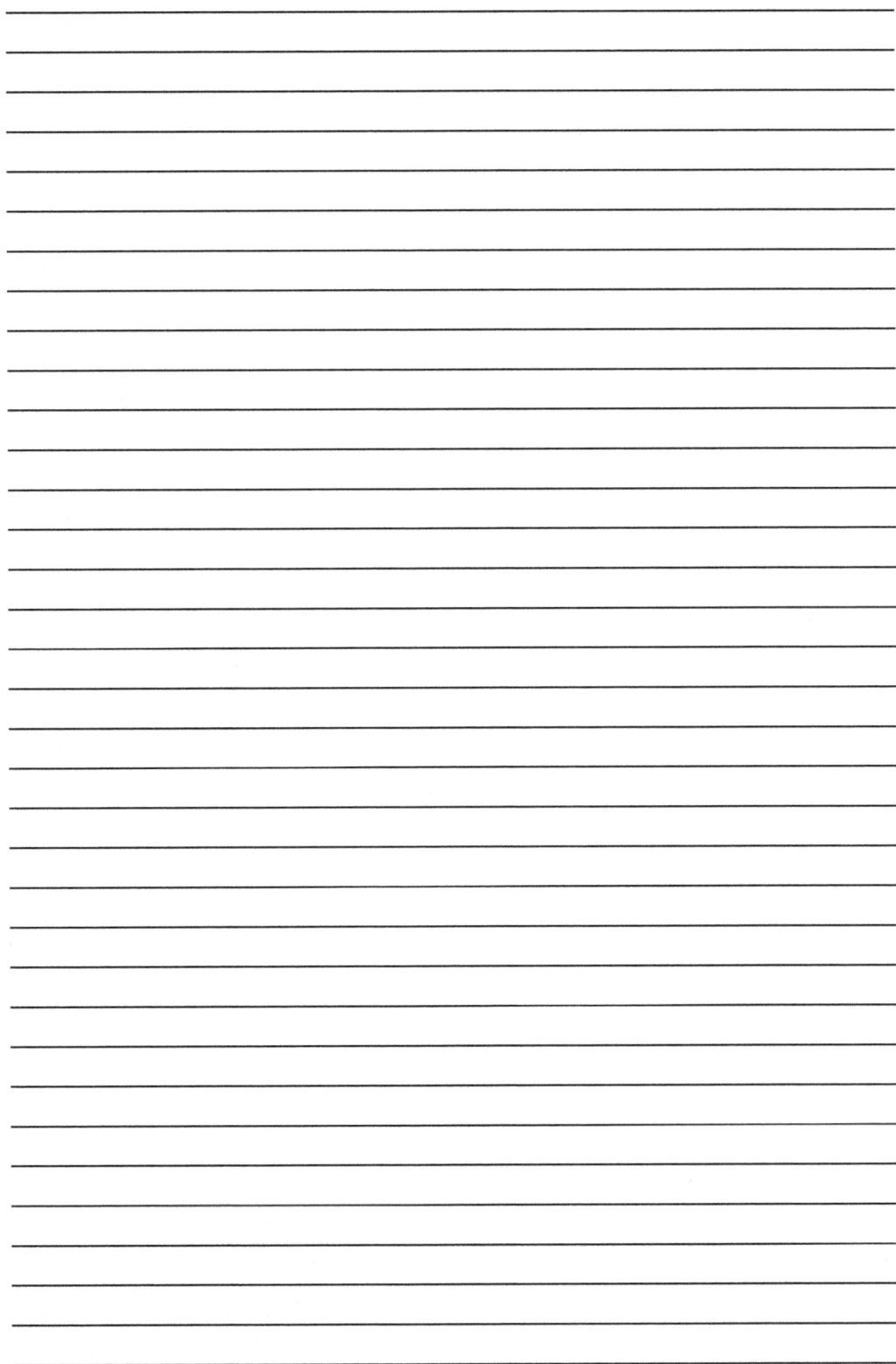

Share an unforgettable dream you once had.

_____

_____

_____

_____

_____

_____

_____

_____

_____

_____

_____

_____

_____

_____

_____

_____

_____

_____

_____

_____

_____

_____

_____

_____

_____

_____

_____

_____

_____

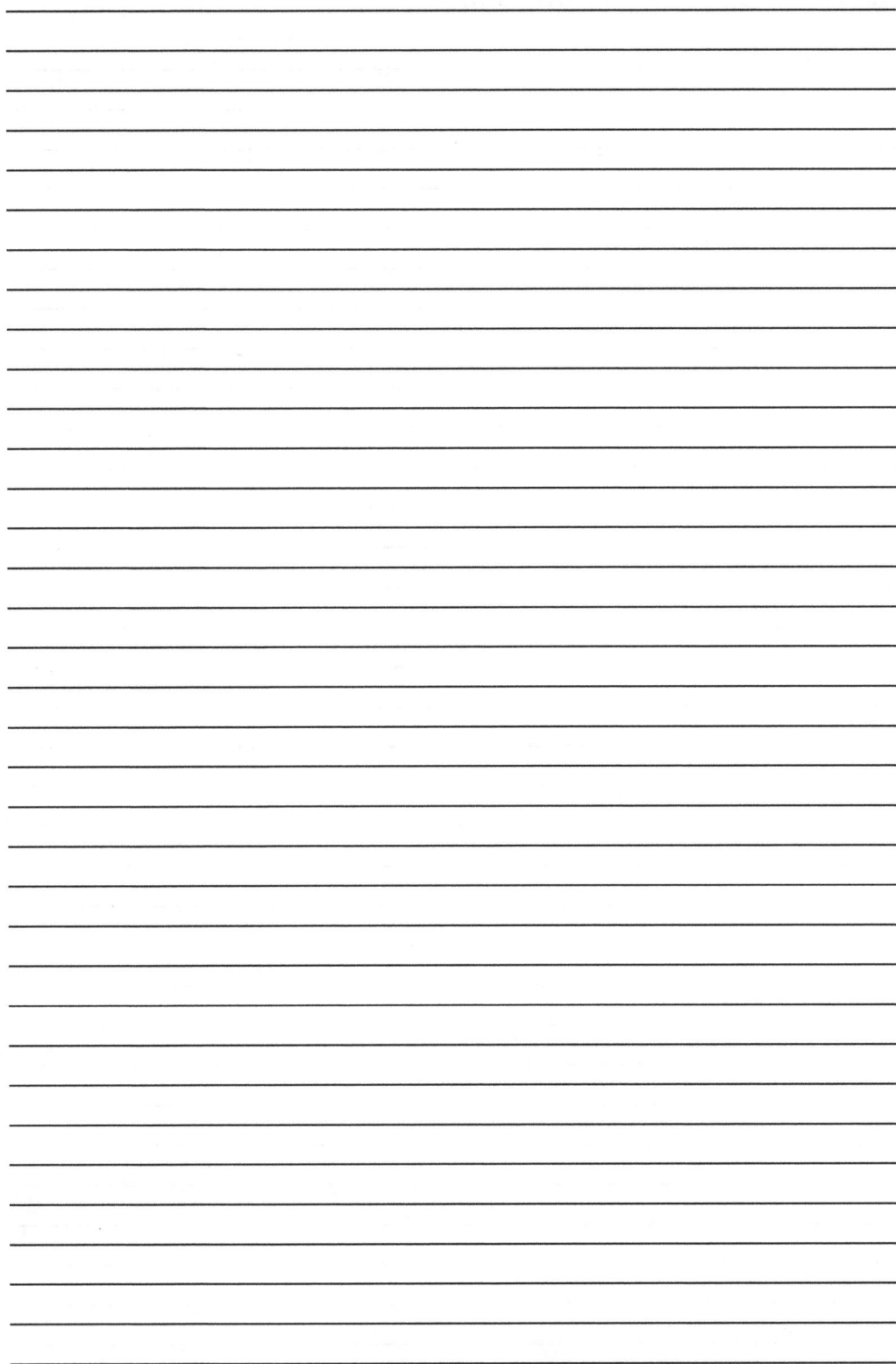

Share anything that you would like.

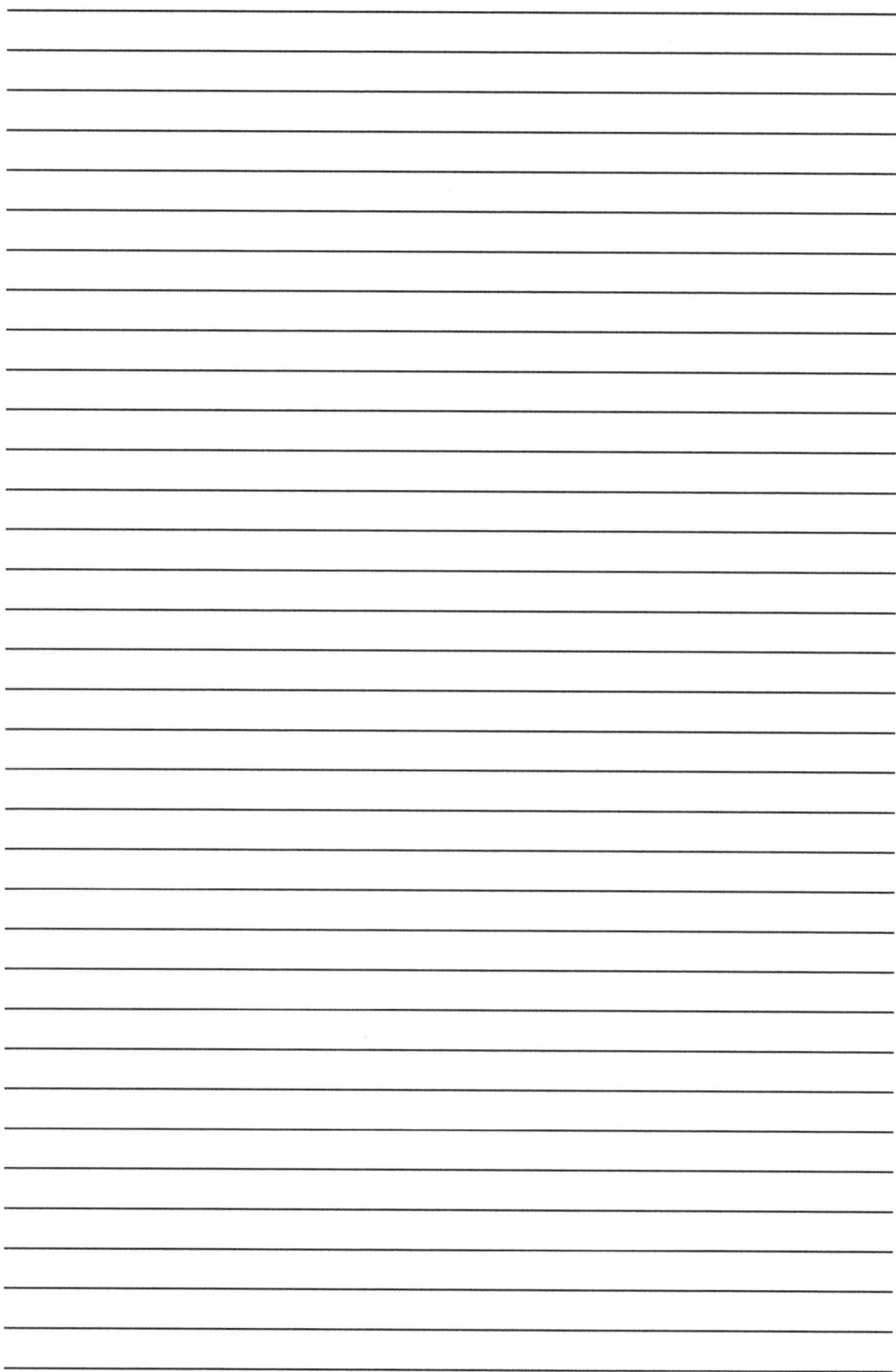

What's Next?

Congratulations! You have written a book and accomplished what many people have only dreamt of doing.

Not only have you written a book but you have penned your memoir. By collecting your personal stories into a single book, you have started the process of saving your greatest legacy, which can be passed onto friends and family.

How can you share this book? Handing the book onto a single friend or family member is one way to share your memories. Another is to include the book in a collection of items as a legacy gift; people may put together a gift package of photos, keepsakes, and other special items to pass on, and your memoir is a perfect addition.

Feel free to distribute your memoir to the people who would cherish your stories. You may be surprised at how many people are interested in reading what you have to say.

If someone in your family enjoys collecting genealogical information on your extended family, be sure this person gets a copy to add to their collection. Your memoir may inspire them to collect stories from other friends and family as part of their genealogical collection.

Can you imagine having a copy of the personal stories from one of your beloved ancestors? This memoir will become a treasured keepsake for your friends and family for generations to come.

www.ingramcontent.com/pod-product-compliance
Lightning Source LLC
Chambersburg PA
CBHW081425090426
42740CB00017B/3190